THE
ESSENTIALS
OF
FINANCE
AND
ACCOUNTING
FOR
NONFINANCIAL
MANAGERS

THE
ESSENTIALS
OF
FINANCE
AND
ACCOUNTING
FOR
NONFINANCIAL
MANAGERS

EDWARD FIELDS

AMACOM
American Management Association

New York • Atlanta • Brussels • Buenos Aires • Chicago • London • Mexico City • San Francisco
Shanghai • Tokyo • Toronto • Washington, DC

Special discounts on bulk quantities of AMACOM books are available to corporations, professional associations, and other organizations. For details, contact Special Sales Department, AMACOM, a division of American Management Association, 1601 Broadway, New York, NY 10019.
Tel.: 212-903-8316   Fax: 212-903-8083
Web site: www.amacombooks.org

This publication is designed to provide accurate and authoritative information in regard to the subject matter covered. It is sold with the understanding that the publisher is not engaged in rendering legal, accounting, or other professional service. If legal advice or other expert assistance is required, the services of a competent professional person should be sought.

Library of Congress Cataloging-in-Publication Data has been applied for and is on record at the Library of Congress.

Printing number

10   9   8   7   6   5   4   3   2   1

Contents

Part 4: Additional Financial Information

Introduction

Background

This is a book for businesspeople. All decisions in a business organization are made in accordance with how they will affect the organization's financial performance and future financial health. Whether your background is marketing, manufacturing, distribution, research and development, or the current technologies, you need financial knowledge and skills if you are to really understand your company's decision-making, financial, and overall management processes. The budget is essentially a financial process of prioritizing the benefits resulting from business opportunities and the investments required to implement those opportunities. An improved knowledge of these financial processes and the financial executives who are responsible for them will improve your ability to be an intelligent and effective participant.

This book is special for a number of reasons:

1. It teaches what accountants do; it does *not* teach how to do accounting. Businesspeople do not need to learn, nor are they interested in learning, how to do debits and credits. They do need to understand what accountants do and why, so that they can intelligently use the resulting information—the financial statements.
2. It is written by a businessperson for other businesspeople. Throughout a lifetime of business, consulting, and training experience, I have provided my audiences with

1

down-to-earth, practical, useful information. I am not an accountant, but I do have the knowledge of an intelligent user of financial statements. I understand your problems, and I seek to share my knowledge with you.

3. It emphasizes the business issues. Many financial books focus on the mathematics. This book employs mathematical information only when it is needed for the business decision-making process.

4. It includes a chapter on how to read an annual report that helps you use the information that is available there to better understand your own company. This chapter also identifies a number of other sources of information in the public domain about your competition that may be very strategically valuable.

5. It includes information on how the finance department contributes to the profitability and performance of the company. The financial staff should be part of the business profitability team. This book describes what you should expect from them.

6. It contains many practical examples of how the information can be used, based upon extensive, practical experience. It also provides several exercises, including a practice case study, as appendices.

The book is in four parts:

Part 1, Understanding Financial Information, Chapters 1 through 5. In Part 1, the reader is given both an overview and detailed information about each of the financial statements and its components. A complete understanding of this information and how it is developed is essential for intelligent use of the financial statements.

Part 2, Analysis of Financial Statements, Chapters 6 through 8. Part 2 describes the many valuable analyses that can be performed, using the information that was learned in Part 1. Business management activities can essentially be divided into two basic categories:

- Measuring performance
- Making decisions

Part 2 describes how to measure and evaluate the performance of the company, its strategic business units, and even its individual products.

Part 3, Decision Making for Improved Profitability, Chapters 9 and 10. This part describes the key financial analysis techniques that managers can use to make decisions about every aspect of their business. Financial analysis provides valuable tools for decision making. However, managers must still make the decisions.

Part 4, Additional Financial Information, Chapters 11 through 13 and appendices. Part 4 provides further information about elements of the financial process that can serve as tools for the business manager. These include the budget and methods of obtaining the financing to support the business. Part 4 also includes a glossary and quite a few practice exercises.

Part 1, Understanding Financial Information

Part 1 discusses the financial reports that the company produces. These include:

- The balance sheet
- The income statement
- The statement of cash flows

Each statement is described, item by item. The discussion explains where the numbers belong and what they mean. The entire structure of each financial statement is described, so that you will be able to understand how the financial statements interrelate and what information they convey.

Part 1 also explains how to read and understand an annual report. The benefits of doing so are numerous. They include:

- Understanding the reporting responsibilities of a public company
- Further understanding the accounting process
- Identifying and using information about your competitors that is in the public domain

Part 2, Analysis of Financial Statements

Now that we have learned how to read the financial statements, we can understand how they are prepared and what they mean. Part 2 describes management tools that help us to use the information in the financial statements to analyze the company's performance. The ratios that will be covered describe the company's:

- Liquidity
- Working capital management
- Financial leverage (debt)
- Profitability and performance

Part 3, Decision Making for Improved Profitability

Part 3 describes a number of tools that can help managers with decision making. It introduces breakeven analysis, which can be used to evaluate individual products and the product mix.

It also explores fixed cost versus variable cost issues within the strategic planning context, such as:

- Supply chain management
- New product strategy
- Marketing strategy

Part 3 also covers return on investment analysis for investment decision making. It explains the principle of discounted cash flow and several methods of analysis that employ it:

- Internal rate of return
- Net present value
- Profitability index

It also discusses ways of integrating profitability requirements with company performance targets and methods of planning and evaluating investments, such as:

- Capital expenditure decisions
- R&D analysis and justification
- Acquiring other companies
- Marketing programs
- Strategic alliances

Part 4, Additional Financial Information

Part 4 describes in considerable detail some additional financial information that will benefit the businessperson. It includes discussions of the planning process and the budget, and why they are so important. It also covers ways of financing the corporation. While this is not a direct responsibility of most members of the management team, knowledge of debt and equity markets and sources of corporate financing is very beneficial.

There are also a number of practice exercises that will reinforce the knowledge gained from the book.

Additional Background

We study financial management because doing so helps us to manage our business more intelligently.

As mentioned earlier, business management activities may be divided into two major categories:

Measuring performance
Making decisions

We measure the performance of products and markets in order to understand the profitability of the business. Knowledge of our company's products, markets, and customers enables us to make decisions that will improve this profitability.

The *income statement* measures the performance of the business for a period of time, usually a year, a quarter, or a month. It enables us to determine trends and identify strengths and weaknesses in the company's performance.

The *balance sheet* measures the financial health of the business at a point in time, usually at the end of a month, quarter, or year. Are we able to finance future growth? Can the company afford to pay off its debt?

Breakeven analysis helps us to understand the profitability of individual products. We can use it to evaluate pricing strategies and costs. The company uses the results of this analysis in decisions concerning outsourcing options, vertical integration, and strategic alliances.

This book surveys these financial tools. We will provide descriptions and definitions of their components and gain an understanding of how they can help us and why we should understand them.

Accounting Defined

Accounting is the process of recording past business transactions in dollars. Training to become a certified public accountant (CPA) involves learning the rules and regulations of the following organizations:

> *The Securities and Exchange Commission.* This is an agency of the federal government that, among other things, prescribes the methodology for reporting accounting results for companies whose stock is publicly traded. Most private companies adhere to most of these rules except for the requirement that they publish the information.
>
> *The Internal Revenue Service.* This agency oversees the filing of all corporate tax reports consistent with the tax legislation passed by the U.S. Congress.
>
> *The Board of Governors of the Federal Reserve System.* This executive branch federal agency prescribes the reporting and accounting systems used by commercial banks.

Two private accounting organizations are integral to the accounting profession:

> *The Financial Accounting Standards Board (FASB).* This is a research organization that evaluates, develops, and rec-

ommends the rules that accountants should follow when they audit a company's books and report the results to shareholders. The products of the FASB's efforts are reports known as *FASB Bulletins.*

The American Institute of Certified Public Accountants. This is the accountants' professional organization (trade association). It is an active participant in the accounting dialogue.

The work of all these organizations and the dialogue among them, along with the work of the tax-writing committees of the U.S. Congress, result in what are known as generally accepted accounting principles.

Generally Accepted Accounting Principles

The concept of generally accepted accounting principles (GAAP) makes an invaluable contribution to the way in which business is conducted. When a CPA firm certifies a company's financial statements, it is assuring the users of those statements that the company adhered to these principles and prepared its financial statements accordingly.

Why Is This Important?

The use of GAAP provides comfort and credibility. The reader of the reported financial statements is typically not familiar with the inner workings of the company. GAAP gives a company's bankers, regulators, potential business partners, customers, and vendors some assurance that the information provided in the company's financial statements is accurate and reliable. It facilitates almost all business dealings.

Why Is This an Issue for the Business Manager?

While accounting principles and practices are critical for the presentation of past history, their mechanics, requirements, and philosophies are not necessarily appropriate when the business manager seeks to analyze the business going forward. To understand this issue, we need to define financial analysis.

Financial Analysis

Financial analysis is an analytical process. It is an effort to examine past events and to understand the business circumstances, both internal and external, that caused those events to occur. Knowing and understanding the accounting information is certainly a critical part of this process. But to fully understand the company's past performance, it is important to also have information concerning units sold, market share, orders on the books, utilization of productive capacity, the efficiency of the supply chain, and much more. Every month, we compare actual performance with the budget. This is *not* an accounting process, it is an analytical process that uses accounting information. Accounting is the reporting of the past. The budget reflects management's expectations for future events and offers a standard of performance for revenues, expenses, and profits.

Financial analysis as a high-priority management process also requires forecasting. A *forecast* is an educated perception of how a decision being contemplated will affect the future of the business. It requires a financial forecast—a financial quantification of the anticipated effect of the decision on marketing and operational events, and therefore on cash flow.

Accounting/Forecasting/Budget Perspective

The end result of all the planning efforts in which a company engages, including forecasting, must be the making of decisions. These many decisions about spending allocations, products, and markets are reflected in a voluminous report called a *budget*. Therefore, the budget is really a documentation of all the decisions that management has already made.

The Issues

There are frequently cultural clashes between the accounting department and the rest of the company. This results from the false assumption that the philosophies and attitudes that are required for accounting are also appropriate in business analysis and decision making. The budget is not an accounting effort. It is a management process that may be coordinated by people with accounting backgrounds. A forecast need not adhere to accounting rules. There is nothing in accounting training that teaches accountants to deal with marketing and operational forecasting and decision-making issues. In addition, to the extent that the future may not be an extension of the past, it is conceivable that past (accounting) events may not be very relevant.

Accounting is somewhat precise. Forecasting, by its very nature, is very imprecise. When the preparation of the budget becomes "accounting-driven," those preparing it focus on nonexistent precision and lose sight of the real benefits of the budget and its impact on the bigger picture.

Accounting is conservative. It requires that the least favorable interpretation of events be presented. Business forecasting needs to be somewhat optimistic. Using a conservative sales forecast usually means that the budget will be finalized at the lower end of expectations. If the forecast is actually exceeded, as it is likely to be, the company will not be totally prepared to produce the product or deliver the services. In short, conservatism in accounting is required. Conservatism in business decision making can be very damaging.

Business is risky and filled with uncertainty. Accounting is risk-averse.

Resolution

To eliminate these cultural clashes, accountants need to learn more about the business—its markets, customers, competitive pressures, and operational issues—and all other business managers need to learn more about the financial aspects of business. This includes the language of accounting and finance, the financial pressures with which the company must deal, and the financial strategies that may improve the company's competitive position, operational effectiveness, and ultimate profitability.

Some Additional Perspectives on the Planning Process

The planning process is a comprehensive management effort that attempts to ensure that the company has considered all of the issues and challenges facing it. The management team will focus on the company's strengths and weaknesses as well as on the resources necessary to properly grow the business compared with the resources available.

The financial team is a critical contributor to this process. The following are some of the issues that require management focus.

The Customers

Why do our customers buy our products and services? Why do we deserve their money? These are critical questions that must be answered if we are to focus our energies and resources on those efforts that will sustain growth. We need to expand our definition of "the highest quality" and devote corporate cash and people to distinguishing our company from and staying ahead of the competition.

Do we really know our customers' needs, present and future? Are we prepared to support them in their goal of succeeding in their marketplace? Do they view us as a key strategic partner? After all, we are in business to help our customers make money. If we define our company's strategic mission accordingly, our customers' success will be ours. What we do is only a means to that end.

The Markets

Products and services are provided in numerous markets. These may be defined by:

- Geography
- Product application
- Quality and perception of quality
- Means of distribution
- Selling channel (direct versus distributor)

The process of thinking through the company's future is an integral part of budget development. It requires that the management team be in touch with trends and developments that will enhance or detract from the company's marketplace position. Periodic "out of the box" reexamination of each of these issues provides considerable opportunity for market and profit improvement.

Resources

People and money must be dedicated to the most profitable, fastest-growing segments of the business. These business segments represent the future of the company and should be properly supported. Are our strategies and practices designed to hang on to the more comfortable past rather than focusing on the future? Intelligent planning and management controls do not inhibit creativity and aggressive risk taking. In fact, they ensure that the most important opportunities receive the resources that they require if they are to succeed.

The Planning Process

The planning process involves the following elements:

1. Thinking through the future of the business
2. Ensuring that members of the management team communicate with one another, so that plans and resources are consistent
3. Researching markets, competitors, and technologies to assure currency of knowledge
4. Deciding among the identified opportunities and programs
5. Implementing those programs that contribute to the company's strategic position and profitability
6. Developing a budget that documents the plan, each of the decisions made, and each department's contribution to achieving company goals
7. Developing intelligent management controls to ensure that the company gets its money's worth

Properly focusing the planning process on the company's strengths and weaknesses will help the company to achieve its strategic and financial goals. If the company truly understands its customers' needs and focuses on helping them to achieve their goals, its progress will continue.

When all of these factors have been put on the table, management must decide what actions should be taken. The financial team helps management to determine:

- How much the programs will cost
- The forecast profitability benefits of the programs
- Whether these forecast achievements are considered excellent
- How much the company can afford

These questions are answered through the financial analysis of each proposal. The company will evaluate the plans using return on investment analysis, which is described in Chapter 10 of this book. Once the decisions are made, they are documented in the budget. The budget identifies what will be achieved, by whom, and how much will be spent.

The financial team will then determine whether the budget is guiding the company toward the achievement of its goals. It will do so through an analysis of the company's ratios. Ratio analysis is described in Chapter 6.

Accountants will then record actual events as they occur each month. As described in Chapter 9, they will then compare the actual revenues and spending with what was budgeted. This is called variance analysis. This same chapter also describes some of the operating decisions that will be made in order to enhance performance and assure budget success.

Since the business environment is constantly changing, financial analysis is an ongoing process. Assumptions must be reviewed frequently, and action plans must be developed in response to changes in these assumptions. Cash must be constantly monitored.

With this perspective on the issues involved, Chapter 1 begins the discussion of the financial statements.

Part 1

Understanding Financial Information

Chapter 1

The Balance Sheet

THE BALANCE SHEET IS A representation of the company's financial health. It is produced as of a specific point in time, usually the end of the fiscal (accounting) year or month. It lists the assets that the company owns and the liabilities that the company owes to others; the difference between the two represents the ownership position (stockholders' equity).

More specifically, the balance sheet tells us about the company's:

Liquidity: The company's ability to meet its current obligations.

Financial health: The company's ability to meet its obligations over the long term; this concept is similar to liquidity except that it takes a long-term perspective. It also incorporates strategic issues.

Financial strength refers to the company's ability to:

- Secure adequate resources to finance its future
- Maintain and expand efficient operations
- Properly support its marketing efforts
- Use technology to profitable advantage
- Successfully compete

The balance sheet also helps us to measure the company's operating performance. This includes the amount of profits and cash flow generated relative to:

- Owners' investment (stockholders' equity)
- Total resources available (assets)
- Amount of business generated (revenue)

By analyzing the data in the balance sheet, we can evaluate the company's asset management performance. This includes the management of:

- Inventory, measured with an inventory turnover ratio
- Customer credit, reflected by an accounts receivable measure known as *days sales outstanding* or *collection period*
- Total asset turnover, which reflects capital intensity, degree of vertical integration, and management efficiency

Mathematical formulas called *ratios* are very valuable in the analytical process. They should be used to compare the company's current performance against:

- Its standards of performance (budget)
- Its past history (trends)
- The performance of other companies in a similar business (benchmarking)

Look at the balance sheet of the Metropolitan Manufacturing Company, shown in Exhibit 1-1, dated as of December 31, 2002. Notice that it also gives comparable figures for December 31, 2001. Providing the information for the prior year is called a *reference point*. This is essential for understanding and analyzing the information and should always be included. The third column gives the differences in the dollar amounts between the two years. This information summarizes cash flow changes that have occurred between December 31, 2001, and December 31, 2002. This very critical information is presented more explicitly in the report called the *sources and uses of funds statement* or the *statement of cash flows*. This is described more fully in Chapter 3. (The numbers in parentheses in the fourth column refer to the lines in Exhibit 3-1, the Sources and Uses of Funds Statement.)

Exhibit 1-1. Metropolitan Manufacturing Company, Inc.
Comparative Balance Sheets
December 31, 2002 and December 31, 2001 ($000)

	2002	*2001*	*Changes*	
1. Cash	$ 133	$ 107	+26	(47)
2. Marketable Securities	10	10		
3. Accounts Receivable	637	597	+40	(43)
4. Inventory	1,229	931	+298	(42)
5. Current Assets	$2,009	$1,645		
6. Investments	59	62	−3	(39)
7. Fixed Assets:				
8. Gross Book Value	$1,683	$1,649	+34	(41)
9. Accumulated Depreciation	(549)	(493)	−56	(35)
10. Net Book Value	$1,134	$1,156		
11. Total Assets	$3,202	$2,863		
12. Accounts Payable	$ 540	$ 430	+110	(37)
13. Bank Notes	300	170	+130	(36)
14. Other Current Liabilities	58	19	+39	(38)
15. Current Portion of Long-Term Debt	0	0		
16. Total Current Liabilities	$ 898	$ 619		
17. Long-Term Debt	300	$ 350	−50	(44)
18. Total Liabilities	$1,198	$ 969		
19. Preferred Stock	150	150		
20. Common Stock	497	497		
21. Retained Earnings	1,357	1,247	+110 ⎱	(34)
			⎰	(45)
22. Stockholders' Equity	$2,004	$1,894		
23. Total Liabilities and Stockholders Equity	$3,202	$2,863		

The numbers in parentheses in the right-hand column refer to the line numbers in Exhibit 3-1, Sources and Uses of Funds.

Expenses and Expenditures

Before we look at the balance sheet in detail, we need to understand the difference between the concepts of expenses and expenditures. Understanding this difference will provide valuable insights into accounting practices.

An *expenditure* is the disbursement of cash or a commitment to disburse cash—hence the phrase *capital expenditure*. An *expense* is the recognition of the expenditure and its recording for accounting purposes in the time period(s) that benefited from it (i.e., the period in which it helped the company achieve revenue).

The GAAP concept that governs this is called the *matching principle:* Expenses should be matched to benefits, which means recorded in the period of time that benefited from the expenditure rather than the period of time in which the expenditure occurred.

The accounting concepts that reflect this principle include the following:

- Depreciation
- Amortization
- Accruals
- Reserves
- Prepaid expenses

Suppose a company buys equipment (makes a capital expenditure) for $100,000. The company expects the equipment to last (provide benefit) for five years. This is called the equipment's *estimated useful life.* Using the basic concept called straight-line depreciation (to be discussed later in this chapter), the depreciation expense recorded each year will be:

$$\frac{\$100,000}{5} = \$20,000$$

Each year there will be an expense of $20,000 on the company's income statement. Clearly during those five years, no such cash expenditures were made.

11. Assets

The assets section of the balance sheet is a financial representation of what the company owns. The items are presented at the lower of their purchase price or their market value at the time of the financial statement (see the discussion of GAAP in Chapter 4). Assets are listed in the order of their liquidity, or the ease with which they can be converted to cash.

1. Cash, $133,000

Cash is the ultimate measure of a organization's short-term purchasing power, its ability to pay its debts and expand and modernize its operations. It represents immediately available purchasing power. This balance sheet category principally consists of funds in checking accounts in commercial banks. This money may or may not earn interest for the company. Its primary characteristic is that it is immediately liquid; it is available to the firm now. This may also be called Cash and Cash Equivalents. Cash equivalents are securities with very short maturities, perhaps up to three months, that can earn some interest income for the company.

2. Marketable Securities, $10,000

This category includes the short-term investments that companies make with cash that will not be needed within the next few weeks or months. As a result of intelligent cash planning, the company has the opportunity to earn extra profit in the form of interest income from these securities. Some companies earn sizable returns on this money through careful cash management and intelligent investment strategies.

The securities that can be placed in this category include certificates of deposit (CDs), Treasury bills, and commercial paper. All have very short maturities, usually 90 to 180 days. CDs are issued by commercial banks, Treasury bills are issued by the U.S. government, and commercial paper is issued by very large, high-quality industrial corporations. Purchasing these high-quality securities, which have little or no risk, gives the company the opportunity to earn a few percentage points on the money it does not need immediately.

3. Accounts Receivable, $637,000

When a company sells products to customers, it may receive immediate payment. This may be done through a bank draft, a check, a credit card, a letter of credit, or in the case of a supermarket or retail store, cash. On the other hand, as part of the selling process, the customer may be given the opportunity to postpone paying for the products or services until a specified future date. This is referred to as giving the customer credit. The accounting term that describes the dollar amount of services provided or products delivered that have not yet been paid for by the customer is *accounts receivable*. This is the amount of money owed to the company for products and services that it has already provided but for which payment has not yet been received. It is expected that this money will be received sometime within a 30- to 60-day time period.

In order to have accounts receivable, the company needs to have achieved *revenue*. Revenue is the amount of money that the company has earned by providing products and services to its customers. Sometimes cash is received before revenue is earned, as when a customer makes a down payment. Retail stores usually receive their cash when they earn the revenue. However, most corporations receive their cash after they earn their revenue, resulting in accounts receivable.

4. Inventory, $1,229,000

This represents the financial investment that the company has made in the manufacture or production (or, in the case of a retail store, the purchase) of products that will be sold to customers. For manufactured goods, this amount is divided in three categories: finished goods, work in process, and raw materials.

Finished Goods. These are fully completed products ready for shipment to customers. The amount shown on the balance sheet includes the cost of purchased raw materials and components used in the products, the labor that assembled the products at each stage of their manufacture (called direct labor), and all of the support expenditures (called manufacturing overhead) that helped to add value to the product. Products in this category continue to be owned by the company, and thus to be assets of the company, until they are delivered to the customer's premises or the customer's distribution network (vehicles, warehouse) and the customer agrees to take responsibility for them (the customer accepts delivery).

Work in Process. Inventory in this category has had some value added by the company—it is more than raw materials and components—but it is not yet something that can be delivered to the customer. If the item has been the subject of any activity by the production line, but is not yet ready for final customer acceptance, it is considered work in process.

Raw Materials. Raw materials are products or components that have been received from vendors or suppliers to which the company has done nothing except receive them and place them into storage for future use. Since the company has not yet put the raw materials into production, no value has yet been added. The amount presented in this category may include the cost of bringing the product from the vendor to the company's warehouse, whether this freight cost is paid separately, itemized in the vendor's invoice, or just included in the purchase price.

5. Current Assets, $2,009,000

This is the sum of the asset classifications previously identified: cash, marketable securities, accounts receivable, and inventory, plus a few other, more minor categories. It represents the assets owned by the company that are expected to become cash (liquid assets) within a one-year period.

Presentation of Current Assets

Accounts receivable is usually presented net of an amount called *allowance for bad debts.* This is a statistically derived estimate of the portion of those accounts receivable that may not be collected. It is based on an analysis of the company's past experience in collecting funds. This estimate is made and the possibility of uncollected funds recognized even though the company fully expects the balance of every individual account in its accounts receivable list to be collected. All of the amounts in the accounts receivable balance were originally credit extended to creditworthy customers who were expected to pay their bills on time—otherwise credit would not have been extended. However, it is possible that some of this money will not be collected.

Allowance for bad debts is usually in the range of 1 to 2 percent of accounts receivable. The amount is determined by the company's internal accounting staff and is reviewed and revised annually within the context of actual collections experience.

For Metropolitan Manufacturing Company, the calculation of net accounts receivable is as follows:

Accounts Receivable	$647,000
Allowance for Bad Debts	(10,000)
Accounts Receivable (net)	$637,000

Accounting for *inventory* also has some specific characteristics of which the reader should be aware.

The figure given for inventory is the amount it cost the company to buy the raw materials and components and to produce the product. The amounts presented are based on the accounting principle *lower of cost or market.* If the economic value of the inventory improves because of selling price increases, because of other market conditions, or because the cost of replacing it has increased, the inventory figure on the balance sheet does not change. Inventory is presented at cost, which is lower than market value at that point in time. However, if the value of the inventory decreases because selling prices are soft or because the prospects for its sale have significantly diminished, then the balance sheet must reflect this deteriorated value. In this case, where market value is below cost, the inventory amounts will be presented at market.

The accounting process necessary to reflect this latter condition is called a *writedown.* The company would be required to write down the value of the inventory to reflect the reduced value.

6. Investments (and Intangible Assets), $59,000

There are a number of possible components of these two categories. They include:

- Ownership of other companies
- Partial equity stakes in other companies, including joint ventures
- Patents
- Trademarks
- Copyrights
- Goodwill

This information is also presented at the lower of cost or market. If the market value of a patent increases by millions of dollars above what the company paid for the right to use it or develop it, this very positive business development will *not* be reflected on the balance sheet. However, if the asset proves disappointing or if it proves to be without value, this must be reflected by a write-down or write-off. It is not the responsibility of accounting to reflect improved economic value of assets, regardless of the business certainty of that improvement.

7. Fixed Assets

Fixed assets are assets owned by the company and used in the operation of its business that are expected to last more than one year. They are sometimes called *tangible assets.* They often represent a substantial investment for the company. Included in this category are:

Land: This land can be the site of an office, factory, or warehouse, or it may be vacant and available for future use.

Buildings: This includes any structures owned by the company, such as factories or other production facilities, offices, warehouses, distribution centers, and vehicle parking and repair facilities.

Machinery and equipment: This category includes all production machinery, office equipment, furniture and fixtures, computers, and any other tangible assets that support the operations of the company.

Vehicles: Trucks (tractors and trailers), company cars used by salespeople or other managers, and rail cars owned by the company are included in this category.

In order to reduce (somewhat) the accounting burden, companies are permitted to identify a threshold amount below which an item will be recorded as an expense on the company's income statement, even though the item is expected to provide benefit for more than one year, is tangible, and therefore would otherwise be considered a fixed asset.

This threshold amount can be as much as several thousands of dollars. Thus, if the company buys a single desk for $1,000, it may be considered an expense and charged to the budget accordingly. However, if the company buys twenty of these desks (and the accompanying chairs), the purchase will be recorded as a capital expenditure and the desks treated as a fixed asset on the balance sheet.

8. Gross Book Value, $1,683,000

This records the original amount paid, at the time of purchase, for the tangible assets that the company currently owns, subject to the lower of cost or market accounting rule. This amount never reflects improved economic value, even if, for example, a piece of real estate was purchased thirty years previously and its market value has greatly increased.

9. Accumulated Depreciation, ($549,000)

This is sometimes called the Reserve or Allowance for Depreciation. It is the total amount of depreciation expense that the company has recorded against the assets included in the gross book value.

When tangible assets are purchased and recorded on the balance sheet as fixed assets, their value must be allocated over the course of their useful life in the form of a noncash expense on the income statement called *depreciation.* When the asset is purchased, its useful or functional life is estimated. Using one of several accounting methodologies, the gross book value is then apportioned over that time period, with the resultant annual amount being called depreciation expense. The accumulated depreciation amount shown on the balance sheet tells us how much has been recorded so far. The concept of an expense being noncash is explored later in this chapter.

10. Net Book Value $1,134,000

This is the difference between the gross book value and accumulated depreciation amounts. It has little, if any, analytical significance.

11. Total Assets $3,202,000

This is the sum total of current assets, the net book value of fixed assets, investments, and any other assets the company may own.

Important Accounting Concepts
Affecting the Balance Sheet

Expense and Expenditure

These are distinctly different concepts. Understanding this will provide valuable insights into accounting practices.

An *expenditure* is the disbursement of cash or a commitment to disburse cash. Hence the phrase "capital expenditure." An *expense* recognizes the expenditure but records it for accounting purposes in the time period(s) that benefited from it, i.e., help the company achieve revenue.

A basic example is a company that in May pays the rent covering the month of June. The expenditure is in May but the expense is in June because that was the period of time that benefited. The GAAP concept that governs this is the *matching principle.* Expenses should be matched or recorded in the period of time that benefited from the expenditure rather than when the expenditure occurred.

The accounting concepts that are affected by this principle include:

- Depreciation
- Amortization
- Accrual
- Reserve
- Prepaid expense

Accounting for Fixed Assets

	Balance Sheet	**Income Statement** (annual expense)	
Year 1			
Gross Book Value	$100,000	Depreciation	$20,000
Accumulated Depreciation	(20,000)	Expense	
Net Book Value	$80,000		
Year 2			
Gross Book Value	$100,000	Depreciation	$20,000
Accumulated Depreciation	(40,000)	Expense	
Net Book Value	$60,000		

In this case, the company makes a capital expenditure of $100,000. The gross book value on the balance sheet will be $100,000. This is a record of what the company paid for the asset when it was purchased. During the first year, the annual depreciation expense on the income statement will be $20,000.

The accumulated depreciation on the balance sheet is the total amount of depreciation expense included on the income statement from the time the fixed asset(s) were purchased. The net book value is the difference between the two.

Notice that the gross book value remains the same in Year 2. This amount may increase if significant enhancements are made to the asset, or it may decrease if the asset's value deteriorates, resulting in a writedown. Generally, however, this amount will remain the same throughout the entire life of the asset.

The accumulated depreciation in Year 2 is the sum total of

the depreciation expenses recorded in Years 1 and 2. It is cumulative.

In Year 5, and for as long after that as the asset is useful, it will remain on the balance sheet as:

Gross Book Value	$100,000
Accumulated Depreciation	(100,000)
Net Book Value	0

The asset no longer has any "book" value. It is said to be *fully depreciated.* Its value to the business, however, may still be substantial. When the asset is ultimately retired, its gross book value, accumulated depreciation, and net book value are removed from the balance sheet.

Depreciation Methods. The most common method of depreciation is called *straight-line.* It basically involves dividing the gross book value by the number of years in the useful life of the asset. In this example, the annual depreciation expense will be:

$$\frac{\$100,000}{5 \text{ years}} = \$20,000$$

There are three other methods that are often used. They are:

- Double-declining-balance
- Sum-of-the-years'-digits
- Per-unit calculation

Double-declining-balance. Notice that in straight-line depreciation, depreciation expense for an asset with a 5-year life is 20 percent times the gross book value. (If the depreciable life were different from 5 years, the calculation would change.) In the double-declining-balance method, the initial calculation is made in the same way (in this case, $100,000 ÷ 5 years = $20,000, or 20 percent of $100,000), but the percentage is doubled, in this case to 40 percent, and the resulting percentage is multiplied by the net book value. The calculation of the depreciation expense based upon a gross book value of $100,000 is as follows:

Depreciation

Year	Expense Net Book Value × 40%	Remaining Balance
1	$100,000 × 40% = $40,000	$100,000 − $40,000 = $60,000
2	$ 60,000 × 40% = $24,000	$ 60,000 − $24,000 = $36,000
3	$ 36,000 × 40% = $14,400	$ 36,000 − $14,400 = $21,600
4	$21,600 ÷ 2 = $10,800	$10,800
5		$10,800
		$100,000

Notice that the first year's depreciation expense is double the amount it would have been using the straight-line method. Also, when the annual expense becomes less than what it would have been under the straight-line method, the depreciation reverts to straight-line for the remaining years. This method is selected by some companies for tax purposes. The first and second years' expense is higher than what straight-line would have yielded, so the tax savings in those years will be higher.

Sum-of-the-years'-digits. In this method, numbers representing the years are totaled, then the order of the numbers is inverted and the results are used to calculate the annual depreciation expense. The calculations are as follows:

$$1 + 2 + 3 + 4 + 5 = 15$$

Year	Annual Expense
1	$100,000 × 5/15 = $ 33,333
2	$100,000 × 4/15 = $ 26,666
3	$100,000 × 3/15 = $ 20,000
4	$100,000 × 2/15 = $ 13,334
5	$100,000 × 1/15 = $ 6,667
	$100,000

This method results in a depreciation expense for the first two years that is higher than the depreciation expense using straight-line but lower than that provided by the double-declining-balance method.

Per-unit. The third depreciation method involves dividing the cost of the fixed asset by the total number of units it is expected to manufacture during its useful life. If a machine is expected to produce 200,000 units of product over its useful life, the per-unit depreciation expense will be calculated as follows:

$$\frac{\$100{,}000}{200{,}000 \text{ units}} = \$ \, 0.50 \text{ per unit}$$

If production during the first year is 60,000 units, the annual expense for that first year will be 60,000 × $ 0.50 = $30,000.

In most manufacturing standard cost systems, the depreciation expense per unit is built into the manufacturing overhead rate or burden.

In all methods of calculating depreciation, accounting principles are not compromised. To summarize:

- Useful life determines the number of years.
- Consistency is required.
- The total of the depreciation expense is usually equal to the original investment.

Accounting for Inventory: LIFO Versus FIFO

Accountants in a company that manufactures or sells products are required to adopt a procedure to reflect the value of inventory. The two procedures that are most commonly used are known as *LIFO* and *FIFO*, which stand for last-in, first-out and first-in, first-out.

You should understand that this is purely an accounting concept. It does not affect the physical management of the product in any way. An example can best illustrate this.

A company purchases 600 units of product at the following prices:

Units	Price	Expenditure
100 units	@ $1.00 each	$ 100.00
200 units	@ $2.00 each	$ 400.00
300 units	@ $3.00 each	$ 900.00
600 units		$1,400.00

Now suppose that 400 units are sold and 200 units remain in inventory. The accounting questions are: What was the *cost* of the goods that were *sold?* And what is the value of the inventory that remains?

Under *LIFO,* the goods that were purchased last are assumed to have been sold first. Therefore, the cost of goods sold (COGS) would be $1,100 and inventory would be $300, calculated as follows:

Cost of Goods Sold:

$$\begin{array}{lll} & 300 \text{ units} \times \$3.00 = \$ 900 \\ & \underline{100 \text{ units} \times \$2.00 = \$ 200} \\ \text{COGS} & 400 \text{ units} = \$1,100 \end{array}$$

Inventory:

$$\begin{array}{lll} & 100 \text{ units} \times \$2.00 = \$200 \\ & \underline{100 \text{ units} \times \$1.00 = \$100} \\ \text{Inventory} & 200 \text{ units} \$300 \end{array}$$

Under *FIFO,* the goods that were purchased first are assumed to have been sold first. Therefore, the cost of goods sold would be $800 and inventory would be $600, calculated as follows:

Cost of Goods Sold:

$$\begin{array}{lll} & 100 \text{ units} \times \$1.00 = \$100 \\ & 200 \text{ units} \times \$2.00 = \$400 \\ & \underline{100 \text{ units} \times \$3.00 = \$300} \\ \text{COGS} & 400 \$800 \end{array}$$

Inventory:

$$200 \text{ units} \times \$3.00 = \$600$$

Companies may also identify the actual cost of each unit, if this can be readily done, or calculate a running average. In this example, if a running average were calculated, the per-unit value of both COGS and inventory would be:

$$\$2.33 = \$1,400/600 \text{ units}$$

This gives a value of $933 for cost of goods sold and $467 for inventory.

18. Liabilities

Liabilities are the amounts that the company owes to others for products and services it has purchased and amounts that it has borrowed and therefore must repay.

Current liabilities include all monies that the company owes that must be paid within one year from the date of the balance sheet. Long-term liabilities are those that are due more than one year from the date of the balance sheet. Included in current liabilities are accounts payable, short-term bank loans, and accrued expenses (which we have included in other current liabilities). There are no issues of quality in these classifications, only time. The current liabilities and current assets classifications are time-referenced.

12. Accounts Payable, $540,000

Accounts payable are amounts owed to vendors or suppliers for products delivered and services provided for which payment has not yet been made. The company has purchased these products and services on credit. The suppliers have agreed to postpone the receipt of their cash for a specified period as part of their sales process. Normally this money must be paid within a 30- to 60-day time period.

13. Bank Notes, $300,000

This amount has been borrowed from a commercial bank or some other lender and has not yet been repaid. Because the amount must be repaid within one year, it is classified as a current liability.

14. Other Current Liabilities, $58,000

This category includes all short-term liabilities not included in other categories; they are primarily the result of accruals. At any given point in time, the company owes salaries and wages to employees, interest on loans to banks, taxes, and fees to outsiders for professional services. For example, if the balance sheet date falls on a Wednesday, employees who are paid at the end of each week have worked for three days as of the balance sheet date, and so the company owes them three days' pay. To reflect the existence of these debts, the company estimates their amounts as of the balance sheet date and records them in an account called accrued expenses. The total amount of these charges is recorded on the income statement as an expense, while the liability for this expense is part of "other current liabilities."

15. Current Portion of Long-Term Debt

This category includes liabilities that had a maturity of more than one year when the funds were originally borrowed, but that now, because of the passage of time, are due in less than one year.

16. Total Current Liabilities, $898,000

This is the total of all the funds owed to others that are due within one year of the date of the balance sheet. It includes accounts payable, short-term loans, other current liabilities, and the current portion of long-term debt.

17. Long-Term Debt, $300,000

Long-term debt is amounts that were borrowed from commercial banks or other financial institutions that are not due until some time beyond one year. Their maturity ranges from just over one year to perhaps twenty or thirty years. This category may include a variety of long-term debt securities, including debentures, mortgage bonds, and convertible bonds. It may also include liabilities to tax authorities, including the IRS, states, and foreign governments.

22. Stockholders' Equity, $2,004,000

Stockholders' equity represents the cumulative amount of money that all of the owners of the business have invested in the business. They accomplished this in a number of ways. Some of them purchased preferred shares from the company. For Metropolitan Manufacturing Company, the cumulative amount that these investors put in is $150,000. Other investors (or perhaps the same people) purchased common shares from the company. The cumulative amount that they put in is $497,000. The third form of investment takes place when the owners of the company leave the profits of the company in the business rather than taking the money out of the company in the form of dividends. The cumulative amount of this reinvestment is represented on the balance sheet by the retained earnings of $1,357,000.

19. Preferred Stock, $150,000

Holders of this class of stock receive priority in the payment of returns on their investment, called *dividends*. Preferred stock carries less risk than common stock (to be discussed next) because the dividend payment is fixed and must be made before any profit is distributed (dividends are paid) to the holders of common stock. Holders of preferred shares will also have priority over common shareholders in getting their funds back if the firm is liquidated in a bankruptcy. The holders of preferred shares are not considered owners of the business. Hence, they generally do not vote for the company's board of directors. However, a corporate charter might provide that they do get to vote if the preferred dividend is not paid for a certain period of time.

Although preferred shares are sometimes perceived as a "debt" of the company without a due date, they are not actually a debt of the company, but rather are part of equity. Because the preferred dividend is not an obligation of the company, unlike the interest paid on long-term debt, these securities are considered to have a higher risk than long-term debt. Because of this higher risk, the dividend yield on preferred stock will usually be higher than the interest rate that the company pays on long-term debt.

20. Common Stock, $497,000

The owners of common stock are the owners of the business. This balance sheet line represents the total amount of money that people have invested in the business since the company began. It includes only those stock purchases that were made directly from the company. The amount shown is the historic amount invested, not the current market value of the shares. In most cases, for each share owned, the holder is entitled to one vote for members of the board of directors. There are some companies that have different classes of common stock with different numbers of votes per share. This explains why some families or individuals are able to control very large corporations even though they actually own a small minority of the shares.

21. Retained Earnings, $1,357,000

Whenever a company earns a profit for the year, the owners are entitled to remove those funds from the company for their personal use. It is, after all, their money. Profits that are distributed to the stockholders are called *dividends*. However, if the business is in need of funds to finance expansion or to take advantage of other profitable opportunities, the owners may leave all or part of their profit in the company. The portion of total profits of the company that the owners have *reinvested* in the business during its entire history is called *retained earnings*.

Collectively, preferred stock, common stock, and retained earnings are known as *stockholders' equity,* or the *net worth* of the business.

23. Total Liabilities and Stockholders' Equity, $3,202,000

On most balance sheets, the accountants will total the liabilities and stockholders' equity. Notice that this amount is equal to the total amount of the assets. While this is something of a format consideration, it does have some significance that we can review here.

The balance sheet equation (Assets − Liabilities = Equity) is always maintained throughout the entire accounting process. This equation is never out of balance. If a company stopped recording transactions at any point in time and added up the numbers, assets minus liabilities would be equal to stockholders' equity.

The balance sheet equation also holds for any business or personal transaction. You cannot buy a house (asset) for $200,000 unless the combination of the amount you can borrow (liabilities) and the amount you have in your own funds (equity) is equal to $200,000.

$$\text{Assets} = \text{Liabilities} + \text{Equity} : \$200,000 = \$150,000 + \$50,000$$

If you can borrow only $150,000 and you don't have $50,000 in cash, you cannot buy the house for $200,000. This analogy is exactly applicable to business transactions and the corporate balance sheet.

Types of Short-Term Debt

Revolving Credit. This is a short-term loan, usually from a commercial bank. While it is often "callable" by the bank at any time, meaning that the bank can require its repayment, it often remains open for extended periods of time. It is usually secured by the company's accounts receivable and inventory. Some banks require that the company pay off this loan for at least one month during the year, probably during its most "cash rich" month. Such a loan may also be called a *working capital loan.*

Zero-Balance Account. This type of short-term working capital loan has a very specific feature: Customer payments go directly to the bank, which uses the funds to reduce the outstanding loan, which benefits the company by reducing its interest expense. When the company writes checks, the bank deposits enough funds in the company's account to cover the payments, increasing the outstanding loan. Hence the checking account always has a zero balance.

Factoring. This is a short-term working capital financing technique in which the company actually sells its accounts receivable to the bank or to a firm called a factoring company. Customers make payments directly to the bank, which actually owns the receivables. This is a fairly expensive form of financing, often costing 2 to 4 percent per month. Sometimes the sale of the accounts receivable is "without recourse." This means that the bank assumes the credit risk of collecting the funds from the company's customers.

Types of Long-Term Debt

There are several kinds of securities that a company can issue in order to acquire debt financing for extended periods of time. The maturity of these securities is always more than one year and can be as much as thirty or forty years, or even longer. The interest on these securities is known as the *coupon rate.*

Debentures. Debentures are corporate bonds whose only collateral is the "full faith and credit" of the corporation. In a bankruptcy, holders of these bonds would be general creditors. Debentures usually pay interest quarterly or semiannually.

Mortgage Bonds. Mortgage bonds are similar to debentures, except that the collateral on the loan is specific assets, usually real estate. The holders of these securities are said to be "secured lenders" because of the specified collateral.

Subordinated Debentures. These are exactly the same as debentures except that, in case of bankruptcy, holders of these securities must wait until all holders of mortgage bonds and debentures have been financially satisfied. Hence their lien on the company's assets is "subordinated."

Convertible Bonds. These bonds are the same as debentures except that their holders have the option of turning them in to the company in exchange for a specified number of shares of common stock (converting them). Because there is an "upside" growth opportunity for holders of this security (since if the price of the company's stock goes up, the shares into which the bond is convertible will increase in value), the coupon rate will usually be much lower than the rate on a regular debenture. The common stock price at which conversion is worthwhile is often called the *strike price*. It is much higher than the stock price at the time the bonds are originally issued.

Zero-Coupon Bond. This is a bond with a long maturity, probably 10 to 20 years. It is very different from other bonds in that the company pays no annual interest. Instead, it sells the bond at a significant discount from full value. Since the buyer receives the full value of the bond at maturity, the buyer is effectively earning "interest" each year as the value of the bond increases. For example, a 10-year, $1,000 bond with a 9 percent interest rate will be sold for $422.40, which is its *present value*, or the amount that, if invested at 9 percent, would equal $1,000 in 10 years. If the buyer holds this bond for 10 years, the company will pay the buyer the full $1,000. The buyer benefits because, in effect, the interest payments are also invested at the coupon rate, in this case 9 percent, and so the effective interest rate will be slightly higher than that on a regular debenture. Pension funds that don't need the annual cash income find this attractive. (However, income taxes may have to be paid on the interest each year, even though no cash is received, so other investors may find this feature less attractive.) The seller enjoys the fact that no annual interest payments need be made, giving the firm many years to grow its business. Of course, the company must repay the full $1,000 at maturity.

Chapter 2

The Income Statement

THE INCOME STATEMENT DESCRIBES THE performance of the company over a period of time, usually a month or a year. Often called a *statement of operations* or a *profit and loss statement (P&L)*, this document measures the company's achievement (revenue) and also the resources (expenses) that were expended in order to produce that achievement. The income statement is summarized as follows:

$$Revenue - Expenses = Profit$$

The difference between revenues achieved and expenses incurred is called *profit* or *net income.*

The following paragraphs describe the details of the income statement. As a reference, we have provided a five-year history of the Metropolitan Manufacturing Company in Exhibit 2-1. This is part of the same set of financials as the balance sheet in Chapter 1. The numbers refer to the line numbers on the income statement.

24. Revenue, $4,160,000

This is the dollar amount of products and services that the company provided to its customers during the year. This is often called *sales;* in Great Britain, it is called *turnover* or *income.* A sale is achieved when the customer takes ownership of and/or responsibility for the products.

Exhibit 2-1. Metropolitan Manufacturing Company, Inc.
Statements of Profit and Loss for the Years Ending December 31,
2002, to December 31, 1998 ($000)

		2002	2001	2000	1999	1998
24.	**Revenue**	**$4,160**	**$3,900**	**$3,800**	**$3,700**	**$3,400**
25.	Cost of Goods Sold	2,759	2,593	2,500	2,420	2,200
26.	Gross Margin	$1,401	$1,307	$1,300	$1,280	$1,200
		34%	**34%**	**34%**	**35%**	**35%**
27.	General and Administrative Expenses	1,033	877	1,025	950	1,000
27a.	EBITDA	368	430	275	350	200
28.	Depreciation	56	50	50	50	45
29.	Net Income Before Tax	$ 312	$ 380	$ 225	$ 280	$ 155
30.	Federal Income Tax	156	190	112	140	78
31.	Net Income	$ 156	$ 190	$ 113	$ 140	$ 77
32.	Cash Dividends	46	46	73	95	40
33.	Change in Retained Earnings	+$ 110	+$ 144	+$ 40	+$ 45	+$ 37

Achieving revenue is quite distinct from "making a sale." You might use the latter phrase when you and the customer agree to terms. You might say that you have made the sale when you receive the purchase order. However, revenue is not recorded until the customer has received and approved of the products or services purchased.

Revenue is the value of products or services that are delivered to a satisfied customer. The customer either pays cash or promises to pay in the future; in the latter case, the amount is recorded as accounts receivable.

Be clear that earning revenue is *not* the same as receiving cash for products and services. Cash can be received prior to the recording of revenue. For example, a customer may make a down payment or deposit or may pay in advance for a magazine subscription. More commonly, however, businesses receive cash after the revenue is earned, resulting in accounts receivable. One type of business in which the receipt of cash and the recording of revenue might occur at the same time is the checkout counter at a supermarket.

The amount of revenue achieved by Metropolitan Manufacturing Company is $4,160,000. This is after reductions for price discounts and allowances for possible returns and warranties. For example:

Gross Amount at List Price	$4,310,881
— Price Discounts	— 86,218 (2.0%)
— Allowances for Returns and Warranties	— 64,663 (1.5%)
= Revenue	$4,160,000

Companies record their revenues in this detail in order to monitor their price discounting practices and other reductions from revenue.

25. Cost of Goods Sold, $2,759,000

Cost of goods sold is the cost of producing or purchasing the goods that are delivered to customers. This amount is subtracted from revenue in order to determine *gross margin* or *gross profit*. Cost of goods sold includes the following elements:

- Raw materials
- Purchased components
- Direct labor (this includes the wages and other payments made to those who actually manufactured the product, and possibly their direct supervisors)
- Operating and repairing the equipment used to manufacture the product
- Other manufacturing expenses, including utilities and maintenance of the production facility

The amount recorded for cost of goods sold is related to the difference between expenses and expenditures, discussed in Chapter 1. Cost of goods sold (an expense) is not the same as cost of production (an expenditure) because of changes in inventory. If inventory levels decrease during the period, then the cost of goods sold will be higher than the cost of production by the amount of the change in inventory.

26. Gross Margin, $1,401,000

This measures the profitability achieved as a result of producing and selling products and services. It measures manufacturing efficiency and the desirability of the company's products in the marketplace. Gross margin percentage is another measure of that performance.

27. General and Administrative Expenses, $1,033,000

This amount represents the cost of operating the company itself. Included in this category are staff expenses (accounting, computer operations, senior management), selling expenses (salaries, travel), promotional expenses (advertising, trade shows) and research and development (technological research).

28. Depreciation Expense, $56,000

This is the portion of prior capital expenditures that has been allocated to the current year and is recorded as an expense in that year. It does not represent a cash expenditure.

29. Net Income Before Tax, $312,000

This amount is equal to revenue minus all operating and nonoperating expenses incurred by the company. For Metropolitan Manufacturing Company, it is:

Revenue	$4,160,000	
− Cost of Goods Sold		2,759,000
− General and Administrative Expenses		1,033,000
− Depreciation Expense		56,000
	$3,848,000	
= Net Income Before Tax	$ 312,000	

30. Federal Income Tax, $156,000

In the United States, corporations pay approximately 34 percent of their profit to the federal government in the form of *income taxes.* For the Metropolitan Manufacturing Company example, however, to simplify the calculations, we used a rate of 50 percent.

31. Net Income, $156,000

This is the amount of profit that the corporation has achieved during the year. All expenses related to purchases from vendors and all other operating expenses have been taken into account. The owners of the business may take this profit for their personal use (dividends) or reinvest all or part of it in the corporation to finance expansion and modernization (retained earnings).

32. Cash Dividends, $46,000

This is the portion of the year's profits that was distributed to the owners of the business. The remainder (the portion that was not paid to the owners) was retained in the business. Therefore:

Net Income	$156,000
− Cash Dividends	46,000
= Increase in Retained Earnings	$110,000

33. Change in Retained Earnings, $110,000

This represents the portion of the profits that the owners reinvested in the business in the year 2002. The cumulative amount that the owners have reinvested in the business since its inception is $1,357,000. This is the cumulative retained earnings; it appears on the balance sheet on line 21. Notice on the balance sheet that line 21 increased by $110,000 in 2002, which represents that year's reinvestment.

Chapter 3

The Statement of Cash Flows

THE THIRD CRITICAL FINANCIAL STATEMENT, along with the balance sheet and the income statement, is called the *statement of cash flows.* In the past it was called the *sources and uses of funds statement,* which is a more accurate description of the information it contains. It describes in summary form how the company generated the cash flows it needed (sources) to finance its various financial opportunities and responsibilities (uses) during the past year. The sources and uses of funds statement for Metropolitan Manufacturing Company is shown in Exhibit 3-1. As you go through it, notice that the line items appear on the balance sheet in the column labeled "Changes." In fact, the sources and uses of funds statement describes the changes in the balance sheet between two successive years, in this case 2002 and 2001. What we will do in this chapter is:

1. Present a sources and uses of funds statement.
2. Discuss the meaning of each number.
3. Describe how each number was developed, relating it back to its source on the balance sheet.
4. Restate the numbers in the statement of cash flows format.

Exhibit 3-1. Metropolitan Manufacturing Company, Inc.
Sources and Uses of Funds for the Year Ending December 31, 2002

Sources of Funds

34. Net Income	$156,000
35. Depreciation	56,000
36. Increase in Bank Notes	130,000
37. Increase in Accounts Payable	110,000
38. Increase in Other Current Liabilities	39,000
39. Decrease in Investments	3,000
40. Total Sources of Funds	$494,000

Uses of Funds

41. Capital Expenditures	$ 34,000
42. Increase in Inventory	298,000
43. Increase in Accounts Receivable	40,000
44. Decrease in Long-Term Debt	50,000
45. Payment of Cash Dividends	46,000
46. Total Uses of Funds	$468,000
47. Net Increase in Cash Balance in 2002	26,000
48. 2001 Ending Cash Balance	107,000
49. 2002 Ending Cash Balance	$133,000

Sources of Funds

34. Net Income, $156,000

The company's profits are a major source of funds. Therefore, net income is traditionally listed first. This number is also the "bottom-line" number in the income statement (line 31). In addition, it strongly affects the retained earnings amount on the balance sheet (line 21). Net income causes retained earnings to increase. Payments of cash dividends cause retained earnings to decrease. Therefore, the $110,000 change in retained earnings (income statement, line 33) is the net of:

Net Income	$156,000	(31 and 34)
− Dividends	− 46,000	(32)
= Change in Retained Earnings	$110,000	(33)

35. Depreciation Expense, $56,000

In a more formal version of this statement, this item would be preceded by the heading "Add Back Items Not Requiring the Disbursement of Cash." The explanation of this is related to the discussion of expenses and expenditures in Chapter 1. When net income was calculated, an expense item was subtracted (line item 28) that did not require a cash expenditure during this period and will never require one in the future. The item is depreciation expense. The expenditures related to this expense—i.e., capital expenditures—have already taken place.

The depreciation expense was subtracted on line 28 for two reasons. First, generally accepted accounting principles (GAAP) require this. Second, depreciation expense is deductible as an expense for corporate income tax purposes, and so including it provides tax benefits. However, for the purposes of the sources and uses of funds statement, it is added back because in terms of cash, it was not a "real" subtraction during this period.

36. Increase in Bank Notes, $130,000

During the year, Metropolitan Manufacturing Company raised $130,000 through additional short-term bank financing. This was added to its previously existing short-term bank debt of $170,000. Notice that Metropolitan added to its short-term debt while also paying off some long-term debt. By its very definition, the long-term amount that was paid off was not due. If it had been due, it would have been classified as "current portion of long-term debt," which is a *current* liability. There could be several explanations for this financing strategy, but it probably was related to the difference between short-term and long-term interest rates. Metropolitan probably borrowed short-term funds at a lower interest rate and used some of the funds to reduce its long-term loan, which had a higher interest rate.

37. Increase in Accounts Payable, $110,000

When a company buys products and services on credit, the purchases are being financed by the supplier, who provides the product or service but does not receive payment for it *at that time.* Overall, an increase in accounts payable shows that the company is making more purchases on credit, and so is being financed by its suppliers to a greater degree. This is not an analysis of the strategy of buying on credit, which considers having vendors finance purchases or extending payment periods to lengthy terms as a cheap source of cash. In an accounting report like this one, it is merely a statement that the amount of accounts payable is larger than in the past. An increase in accounts payable can result from the following actions:

- Taking more time to pay bills
- Buying more products on credit
- Paying higher prices for credit purchases

38. Increase in Other Current Liabilities, $39,000

Any increase in a liability is a source of funds. Since this category is primarily made up of accruals and similar items, it naturally increases each year as the company gets larger.

39. Decrease in Investments, $3,000

The company sold some investments that were on the books for $3,000. These investments could have been bonds, long-term certificates of deposit, or possibly the common stock of another company.

40. Total Sources of Funds, $494,000

This is the sum of:

Net Income	$156,000
Depreciation	56,000
Increase in Bank Notes	130,000
Increase in Accounts Payable	110,000
Increase in Other Current Liabilities	39,000
Decrease in Investments	3,000
	$494,000

Uses of Funds

41. Capital Expenditures, $34,000

The company used $34,000 to add to its fixed assets. This is evidenced by the increase in the gross book value of fixed assets. Since assets are presented at the lower of cost or market, the only explanation for an increase in gross book value is the purchase of fixed assets.

42. Increase in Inventory, $298,000

While inventory is sold and replenished many times during the course of the year (this is discussed further in Chapter 6), on a net basis, Metropolitan has invested an additional $298,000 in inventory. The increase in the level of inventory could be the result of any combination of the following:

- Replacement costs are greater than the cost of what was sold.
- Costs have remained the same, but the number of units in inventory has increased.
- The mix of products on hand has changed in the direction of more expensive products.

It cannot be determined simply from the inventory numbers whether inventory increased because sales forecasts were overly optimistic or sales were disappointing. We do not know if it was raw materials, work in process, or finished goods inventory that increased. Analysis of these issues will be necessary. The only thing that is certain is that the financial investment in inventory has increased.

43. Increase in Accounts Receivable, $40,000

The company has "invested" this additional amount in financing its customers. This many be the result of any of the following:

- Higher sales levels
- More generous credit terms
- A deterioration in collection performance

Providing customers with credit is a marketing investment that, the company hopes, will produce more and happier customers who purchase more product. However, not enforcing credit agreements is a sign of either accounting sloppiness or marketplace weakness (fear that customers would not buy if they could not take their time in paying).

44. Decrease in Long-Term Debt, $50,000

Metropolitan Manufacturing Company *used* $50,000 to reduce its long-term debt. The rules of accounting provide strong evidence that this was a voluntary act. Long-term debt by definition is not due within the current year. As mentioned in the discussion of the increase in short-term debt, if this amount had been due, it would have been classified as a current liability, most likely *current portion of long-term debt*. This payment could have been made because of any combination of the following:

- The interest rates on the long-term debt were high.
- The company had extra cash.
- The company used the proceeds from lower-cost short-term bank debt.

45. Payment of Cash Dividends, $46,000

The board of directors of Metropolitan Manufacturing Company voted to pay the holders of preferred and common shares cash dividends amounting to $46,000. Such dividends are traditionally but not necessarily voted on and disbursed on a quarterly basis.

Notice that Retained Earnings on the balance sheet (line 21) was affected by two activities, net income and cash dividends, as follows:

Retained Earnings, 12/31/01		$1,247,000
Plus: Net Income, 2002	$156,000	
Minus: Cash Dividends, 2002	− 46,000	
Equals: Change in Retained Earnings, 2002		$110,000
Retained Earnings, 12/31/2002		$1,357,000

46. Total Uses of Funds, $468,000

This is the sum of:

Capital Expenditures	$34,000
Increase in Inventory	298,000
Increase in Accounts Receivable	40,000
Decrease in Long-Term Debt	50,000
Payment of Cash Dividends	46,000
	$468,000

47. Cash Reconciliation

Beginning Cash Balance		$107,000
Plus: Sources of Funds:	$494,000	
Minus: Uses of Funds:	− 468,000	
Equals: Increase in Cash		+ 26,000
Ending Cash Balance:		$133,000

Statement of Cash Flows

Accounting reports require a specific format for this information that is different from the more analytical format presented here. This format, called the *statement of cash flows,* will be found in all published annual reports of public companies, and also in the financial reports of almost every other company whose financials are prepared and produced by certified public accountants. The information is presented in three sections:

Cash flows provided by/used for operations
Cash flows provided by/used for investments
Cash flows provided by/used for financing

It is important to be familiar with and understand this format because most financial information that is available is presented in this way. Note that uses of funds are shown in parentheses ( ) and that sources of funds are shown without parentheses. The statement of cash flows for Metropolitan Manufacturing Company is shown in Exhibit 3-2.

Financial Review

Before you begin the process of analyzing the data provided, it would be very useful for you to review the content and structure of the financial statements. To accomplish this, complete the financial statement exercise in Appendix A.

Exhibit 3-2. Metropolitan Manufacturing Company, Inc.
Statement of Cash Flows for the Year Ending December 31, 2002

Net Income	$156,000	
Depreciation	56,000	
Increase in Inventory	(298,000)	
Increase in Accounts Receivable	(40,000)	
Increase in Accounts Payable	110,000	
Increase in Other Current Liabilities	39,000	
Cash Flow Provided by (Used for) Operations		**$ 23,000**
Capital Expenditures	($ 34,000)	
Sale of Investments	3,000	
Cash Flow Provided by (Used for) Investments		**($ 31,000)**
Increase in Bank Debt	$130,000	
Decrease in Long-Term Debt	(50,000)	
Payment of Dividends	(46,000)	
Cash Flow Provided by (Used for) Financing		**$ 34,000**
Net Cash Increase		$ 26,000
Add: Beginning Cash Balance		107,000
Cash at End of Year		$133,000

Chapter 4

Generally Accepted Accounting Principles: A Review

THE ROLE OF THE FINANCIAL Accounting Standards Board (FASB) was briefly described in the introduction. This is a research organization, made up primarily of accountants. The FASB, along with the entire accounting profession, has, over time, developed a series of rules called *generally accepted accounting principles (GAAP)*. In addition, the FASB publishes what are called *FASB Bulletins.* These are a series of more than one hundred publications that describe what corporate reporting methodologies should be. Most of these methodologies have been adopted and are now incorporated into accounting practice. A broad analogy is that the GAAP rules are the basic constitution and the bulletins are proposed amendments. Here are some of the GAAP rules.

The Fiscal Period

All reporting is done for predetermined periods of time. Reports may be issued for months or quarters and certain reports are issued annually. Accounting fiscal periods usually coincide with calendar periods, although not necessarily with the calendar year. For example, a company's *fiscal year* may be July 1 to June 30 or February 1 to January 31.

The Going Concern Concept

When accountants are keeping the books and preparing the financial statements, they presume that the company will continue to be in existence for the foreseeable future. If there is serious doubt about this, or if the company's ceasing operations is a certainty, the financial statements (essentially the balance sheet) will be presented at estimated liquidation value.

Historical Monetary Unit

Accounting is the recording of *past* business events in dollars. Financial statements, and in fact all financial accounting, report only in dollars. While units of inventory, market share, and employee efficiency are critical business issues, reporting on them is not within the realm of financial accounting responsibility.

Financial statements depicting past years are presented as they occurred. The selling prices of the products and the value of assets may very well be different today, but reports of past periods are not adjusted.

Conservatism

The principle of conservatism requires that "bad news" be recognized when the condition becomes possible and the amount can be estimated, whereas "good news" is recognized only when the event (transaction) has actually occurred.

One example of this is the allowance for bad debts on the balance sheet, which is recorded before the losses are actually incurred. Another example is reserves for inventory writedowns, which are recorded before the dated or out of style products are actually put up for sale at distress prices. Revenue, however, is not recorded, no matter how certain it is from a business point of view, until the product is actually delivered or the service is actually provided. Payment in advance, while assuring the certainty of the sale in a business sense, does not change the accounting rule. Revenue is recorded only when it is earned.

Quantifiable Items or Transactions

The value of the company's workforce and the knowledge the workers possess may in a business sense be the company's critical competitive advantage. However, because that value cannot be quantified and expressed in dollars, accounting does not recognize it as an asset. The value of trademarks and franchise names is also generally not included. Coke, Windows, and Disney are certainly franchise brand names with worldwide recognition. While the business value of a franchise name can be almost infinite if it is maintained, franchise names are not assets on the balance sheet because that value cannot be quantified.

Consistency

Accountants make many decisions when they are preparing the company's financial statements. These include but are not limited to the choice of depreciation method for fixed assets and the choice of LIFO or FIFO accounting for inventory. Once these decisions have been made, however, later successive financial statements must employ the same methodology. When a major change is made in accounting methodology, the accountants must highlight that change and redo past financial statements (the reference points) to reflect that change. Only then can comparative analysis and trends be valid.

Full Disclosure

When a major change in methodology occurs, accountants must take steps to be certain that readers of the financial statement are fully aware of that change and how it affected the financial results.

Materiality

An event that is material, or significant, is one that may affect the judgment, analysis, or perception of the reader of the information. Events that are perceived as *material* must be disclosed separately and highlighted accordingly. This is a relative concept. Something that is significant in a company with annual revenues of $20 million might be largely irrelevant in a multibillion-dollar enterprise.

Chapter 5

The Annual Report and Other Sources of Incredibly Valuable Information

EVERY ANALYST AND BUSINESS MANAGER should be intimately acquainted with the information in the public domain that they can access and use for a variety of purposes. Sources cited here will include:

- The annual report
- The 10K report to the Securities and Exchange Commission
- The Public Register, Morningstar
- The *Wall Street Journal*
- *Forbes* and *Fortune* magazines and their Web sites

There is an enormous amount of valuable information available that everyone should be aware of. Much of it is free.

The Annual Report

The annual report should be read for the many valuable insights it provides:

1. It is a wonderful review of the accounting process and the concept of generally accepted accounting principles (GAAP).
2. There is much that you can learn about your own company from its annual report. This includes how it perceives itself and how it presents itself to the rest of the world.
3. The information contained in your competitors' annual reports provides valuable insights into their financial condition, performance, and strategies.

Background

The company used as the primary subject of this discussion is DuPont Inc, based in Wilmington, Delaware. This company was founded in the United States in 1802. Its European predecessor company is even older. Other companies whose annual reports are referred to in this discussion are the Walt Disney Company and Merck. Each of these companies must prepare an annual report and send a copy to each shareholder because its shares are registered with the Securities and Exchange Commission and are publicly traded. Not all companies are subject to SEC regulation; only those whose shares are registered and publicly traded are subject to them. The size of the company is not an issue here; some very large (multibillion-dollar) companies are private, and some very small companies have publicly traded shares.

The annual report is a product of many regulatory requirements, serves as a public relations vehicle, and reflects strong tradition. Many companies include information in their annual report that is not specifically required. However, because that information has historically been presented every year, it becomes expected, and omitting it would arouse questions.

Dupont used to be called DuPont Chemical Company. The cover of its 1998 report provides an announcement of a very strategic repositioning:

> DuPont is a science company. We bring science to the marketplace in ways that benefit people and generate value for our shareholders.

This is an announcement to:

1. *The public.* Science has a positive image; chemicals do not.
2. *Its employees.* DuPont has always been in the forefront as a "knowledge" company. This emphasizes that orientation.
3. *Security analysts.* Science companies are much more attractive to investors than chemical companies. DuPont has been successfully changing its mix of products. Its stock will perform better if security analysts and investors know of and believe in this repositioning strategy. Science companies are known for higher margins and higher growth. The analysts will assume that DuPont can support a higher price/earnings ratio if it is perceived as a science company.

The inside cover of the annual report provides a highlights section. It includes summary financial information from the income statement and balance sheet along with stock market data—earnings per share and stock prices. DuPont spends over $1 billion a year for research and development and averages more than $5 billion a year in capital expenditures and acquisitions of other companies. The company is (and wants us to know that it is) dedicated to knowledge and is a modern and efficient business.

CEO's Letter to Shareholders

The chief executive officer is required to write a letter to shareholders. This letter includes a description and analysis of all business events of the past year that have had a significant (read material) impact on the performance and condition of the company. It also includes considerable commentary on how the company sees its future.

This letter is reviewed as part of the audit process. It must present all issues in an even-handed manner. Negative as well as positive events must be presented in a logical, cohesive way so that the reader will learn useful information. Bad news is often presented early in this letter so that the positive corrective actions that are already in process can be described. The company wants to convey the idea that management is on top of things and knows what has to be done. Management's credibility is at stake.

In recent years, DuPont has made a major divestiture, of Conoco Oil Company, for which it received more than $4 billion in cash. It has also invested heavily in pharmaceutical businesses. This supports its strategic repositioning away from resources and commodities and toward the sciences. Its businesses now include materials, chemicals, and biological products. The company's history of innovation includes the invention of nylon. Management hopes that this tradition of innovation will continue.

This letter was written by a team whose profession is described as "financial public relations." This internal team, supported by outside consultants, is responsible for all phases of DuPont's relationship with its investors and others who are interested in its financial performance; their responsibilities include the annual report presentation, shareholders' meetings, communication with security analysts, and general communications. The letter is audited by the company's outside CPA firm to assure its compliance with GAAP, its accuracy, and its fairness.

Public Relations

Large companies like DuPont have a multitude of interlocking constituencies. The stockholders, some of whom are often employees, are the voters who elect the board of directors, which in turn appoints the officials responsible for regulatory issues, including taxes, corporate governance, relationships with the Food and Drug Administration (FDA), and environmental concerns. The annual report is also a presentation to the company's customers, some of whom may be stockholders. DuPont wants to influence the way it is viewed by the world. To accomplish this, it devotes more than ten pages to a description of each of its businesses. The photographs included are intended to convey the idea that the employees shown are "just people," building shareholder value by helping "other people." The choice of photographs (and the decision to include them at all) is motivated by public relations considerations and supports the image the company is trying to present.

· The CEO's letter in the 1999 annual report of the Walt Disney Company has some interesting features. It is addressed to "Disney Owners and Fellow Cast Members." Employees of all Disney theme parks are known as cast members. This letter indicates that the company holds those cast members in very high esteem. It presents, in a very direct manner, some very pointed themes.

1. *Revitalizing underperforming areas (home video and consumer products).* Right up front, the letter describes an issue in cliché terms and then identifies the focus of the comment. Disney is focusing on some issues to address and wants us to know that it knows that these issues need to be addressed.
2. *Achieving greater profitability from existing assets (controlling costs).* The letter describes the need for greater efficiency and indicates that the company need not remain in all its current businesses forever. The company's strategic sourcing program means more pricing and service cooperation from vendors who seek to continue in that capacity.
3. *Capital efficiency initiatives to drive long-term growth (how best to invest).* Disney has included outside partners in many of its ventures and to some extent is becoming a theme park management company. This provides more focus on and cash from its core competencies.
4. *Continued product development (being Disney).* Disney is an entertainment company that is quite successful in its cross-branding strategy. Its parks, cruises, movies, TV and cable, and consumer products mostly carry the Disney brand and cross-sell one another.

Management Discussion and Analysis

This section of the annual report provides an extensive, somewhat detailed review of the past year. In paragraph form, the company discusses its financial results in considerable detail.

DuPont presents considerable information about the results of each of its business units. This is referred to as *segment reporting*.

Many years ago, when companies diversified into somewhat unrelated businesses, it became difficult for analysts to benchmark these companies against their competitors because their business identity was difficult to determine. The result was a requirement that a company include in its annual report financial information for each of its business segments. The latest accounting document that specifically requires this information is called Statement of Financial Accounting Standards (SFAS) No. 131. It is entitled "Disclosures About Segments of an Enterprise and Related Information." The resistance on the part of companies to providing this information stems from the companies' desire to avoid providing competitors with valuable information. While segment reporting provides only summary information, it is competitively valuable. DuPont's segments are:

- Agriculture and nutrition
- Nylon enterprise
- Performance coatings and polymers
- Pharmaceuticals
- Pigments and chemicals
- Polyester enterprise
- Specialty fibers

DuPont provides revenue and operating income figures for each segment and discusses the outlook for the future for each division. In addition, information is available that considers the assets dedicated to each segment and gives some measure of the segments' technology investment. In the pharmaceutical area, DuPont gives us its assessment of the probable success of each of the company's research efforts that is in one of the various phases of clinical trials. It would be interesting to get an assessment of the record of success in clinical trials of DuPont's pharmaceutical competitors. DuPont also reveals that the risk-adjusted hurdle rate the company uses to evaluate capital expenditures is 15 percent. The significance of this is discussed in Chapter 10 of this book.

For the company as a whole and for each segment, the annual report provides a considerable amount of information about the company's expectations for the future. This part of the report is called an *outlook*. Management must be very careful about this presentation. It might cause existing and potential investors to make decisions about their investments in the company that may have an undesirable outcome. If this discussion is handled correctly, the company cannot be blamed for this, because it is not giving advice; it is merely presenting management's assessment of the future. It provides disclaimers for this outlook and carefully states that the company cannot be held responsible for the outlook's accuracy.

Disney's annual report makes a very clear distinction between management's outlook for the future and outright prediction and advice. It makes the following statement:

> The Private Securities Reform Act of 1995 (the Act) provides a safe harbor for forward-looking statements made by or on behalf of our company. The company and its representatives may from time to time make written or oral statements that are "forward-looking." . . . Management believes that all statements that express expectations and projections with respect to future matters, including . . . are made on the basis of management's views and assumptions, as of the time the statements were made, regarding future events and business performance. There can be no assurance, however, that management's expectations will necessarily come to pass.

This is very often referred to as "safe harbor." Management is trying to give the readers of the annual report its view of the company's future. It is very even-handed in discussing the company's weaknesses as well as its strengths. Management is rightly protected from litigation over these views; if it were not, it could not afford to take the risk of presenting its assessment. The annual report would become exclusively a compliance document that would contain much less valuable information and would provide no sense of the company's future. Imagine the political and legal issues that would arise if the company had to publish its budget. The lawsuits would be unwieldy if the company didn't make its numbers. They might even be worse if actual performance exceeded budgeted projections. Therefore, management simply discusses the company's future in general terms and is protected from litigation when it does so. No forecast numbers are provided, and rightly so. Only strategies and issues are included in the discussion.

With this in mind, consider using your competitors' annual reports to learn about their strategies and issues.

Report of Independent Accountants

This is a letter written by the company's outside accounting firm. It is addressed to the stockholders of the company, to whom the accounting firm reports, and sometimes also to the board of directors. When the company sends out the notice of the annual meeting, it will include a proxy statement that identifies the major issues that will be decided by shareholder vote at the annual meeting. If a shareholder does not attend the meeting, the shareholder's vote is not sacrificed. Rather, the shareholder may vote by "proxy." (This effectively means that the shareholder may vote by mail.) One of the questions on the proxy statement is whether the stockholders approve (or not) of the board of directors' recommendation to renew the contract of the outside CPA firm or to appoint a different CPA firm. The vote almost always confirms the board's recommendation. No alternative CPA firm is presented. However, in circumstances where there have been extreme problems with the audit process or with accounting integrity, the stockholders, in this somewhat democratic process, do have the ability to discontinue the CPA firm's services.

The Audit Process. The company's internal accounting staff is responsible for "keeping the books" and producing the financial statements. Larger companies have an organization called internal audit that is separate from the accounting staff and, to some degree, reviews the accounting staff's work. The 1999 annual report of Merck describes the role of the internal auditors very well:

> To assure that financial information is reliable and assets are safeguarded, management maintains an effective system of

> internal controls and procedures . . . an organization that provides appropriate division of responsibility, and communications aimed at assuring that Company policies and procedures are understood throughout the organization. . . . A staff of internal auditors regularly monitors the adequacy and application of internal controls on a worldwide basis. (p. 56)

While these internal auditors are employees of Merck, they function as surrogates for the outside CPA firm and support the external auditing efforts. Merck's outside CPA firm is Arthur Andersen, LLP. DuPont and Disney use PricewaterhouseCoopers, LLP. These are both multinational CPA firms with offices in most parts of the world and thousands of partners.

Auditors ensure that transactions were recorded correctly. They verify the accuracy of the financial statements and the many estimates that were made by management. All publicly traded companies in the United States are required to have their financial statements audited. Most large private companies have their financial statements audited, as well. This process is becoming global, as it facilitates international transactions and ventures.

The Letter. The CPA firm writes a letter to the stockholders. Most companies' letters are the same, but the letter reveals some very interesting information about the accounting process. It is worthwhile to cite Merck's 1999 letter:

> We have audited the accompanying consolidated balance sheet of Merck & Co . . . and related consolidated statements of income, retained earnings . . . and cash flows for each of the three years. . . . These financial statements are the responsibility of the Company's management. Our *responsibility* is to express an *opinion* on these financial statements based upon our audit.
>
> We conducted our audit in accordance with auditing standards generally accepted in the United States. Those standards require that we plan and perform the audit to obtain reasonable *assurance* about whether the financial statements are free of material misstatement. An audit includes

examining, on a *test basis,* evidence supporting the amounts and disclosures in the financial statements. An audit also includes assessing the accounting principles used and significant *estimates* made by management

This letter has some very interesting features that provide insights into the accounting and audit processes. The first sentence makes it very clear what role Arthur Andersen played: It audited. The next statement confirms that Merck is responsible for the numbers. Arthur Andersen expresses an *opinion* on the financial statements. This is a very simple term that has been the subject of an incredible amount of controversy over the years. The letter does not refer to a warranty or fact. That is why this letter is often called "the opinion letter." Arthur Andersen uses the term *assurance* later in the letter, just to reinforce its role.

Notice that Arthur Andersen examined the numbers "on a test basis." The auditing firm does not verify every item in the books. Instead, it uses samples: it selects a certain fraction of the company's customers to confirm accounts receivable, selects a certain fraction of vendors to confirm payables, and uses similar measures to confirm payroll, inventory, and all other significant (read material) items. The burden is on Merck to prove that assets are listed at the lower of cost or market and that all other accounting principles have been adhered to.

The last statement in the letter confirms that the financials reflect *estimates.* Depreciation expense is based upon the estimated number of years that the machinery will last. Reserve for bad debts is an estimate of the portion of the accounts receivable that will not be collected. The pension fund calculation is based upon projections of how much employees will have earned when they retire and how many employees will be eligible. These estimates are based on the best available information, but they are nonetheless estimates.

After all of the accounting and auditing work has been done, the CPA firm will provide one of three responses. An *unqualified opinion* really means an opinion without qualification or reservation. It indicates that the company being audited has done a very good job in keeping its books and preparing its financial statements in accordance with generally accepted accounting principles.

A *qualified opinion* means that everything is fine, with one exception. The company and the CPA are generally in agreement, but they have "agreed to disagree" on one aspect of the presentation. This is usually an interpretation of a GAAP issue or the accounting for a single business event, such as the purchase or sale of a business. The letter will describe the auditors' position on the issue in question. If the client company is in serious financial trouble, to the point that its continuance as an ongoing business is in question, the audit letter will also discuss this issue.

No opinion or an *adverse opinion* results when the accounting books are in such disarray that the auditors cannot confirm the numbers. Control procedures may be poor or absent. Accounting irregularities will certainly trigger this result, as will a pattern of not adhering to GAAP. As a general rule, changing CPA firms is not something that a major company does casually. The relationship between the company and the firm has been built up over many years and involves a considerable degree of cooperation and trust. If the CPA firm resigns or is asked to do so, this is usually evidence of severe disagreements over the accounting process or reporting of results. It's much easier for the CPA firm to reassign accountants than to lose a client if personality or culture is an issue.

Footnotes

The footnotes to the financial statements are a critical part of the annual report presentation and also contain some useful information:

1. We can learn more about the company's acquisition, divesture, and strategic alliance efforts. There may be possible clues to the company's strategic direction. Prices of transactions are sometimes included.
2. We can see how the company manages the risk associated with being global. For example, Merck provides an analysis that includes currency rates, commodity prices, and interest rates.
3. We can learn what lines of credit the company has and

what interest rates it is paying on debt securities and earning on its investments in marketable securities.

4. We can learn how the company deals with legal and environmental issues. For example, Phillip Morris's annual report has an extensive description of the tobacco lawsuits.

5. From the segment reporting section, we can determine the key ratios for each of a company's businesses. This can be an excellent way for you to focus in on those segments against which you compete.

Other Important Information in the Annual Report

1. Financial and statistical information for five or ten years is often included. This provides a valuable overview of the company's performance and its consistency. It is interesting to compare the ten-year history with the behavior of the U.S. and global economies during the same period. This may provide some indication of how economic events affect the company and how the company deals with this environment.

2. A list of the management team and the board of directors is given. Which executives are invited to join the board may provide an indication of the company's succession plans. Outside directors who are or were CEOs of other companies may become candidates for the top job at this company if the management team does poorly and an outside perspective is required.

3. The annual report also provides certain corporate information that appears to be routine. Somewhere at the back there appears a section that includes:

   - The place and time of the annual meeting
   - How to get a 10K report
   - How to contact various departments in the company with questions
   - Whether the company has dividend reinvestment and direct stock purchase programs
   - How to get additional information

These don't seem like startling bits of information, but achieving these stockholder rights required many years of effort from many people. Company management used to be a "closed system" in many cases. Shareholders had very few rights other than the right to sell their shares if they were not happy with their investment. What happened over time was the development of a group of people known as *shareholder activists.* It would be reasonable to assume that company managements used descriptions of these people that were much less friendly. For a long-term perspective on this movement, every businessperson should know about the Gilbert brothers, John and Lewis (see sidebar).

The Gilbert Brothers— The Original Shareholder Activists

Background

If you saw the movie *Wall Street,* you saw Michael Douglas as Gordon Giecko browbeat the board of directors of a multinational company because the directors were arrogant and detached from the needs of the stockholders and the company. They were making big salaries and bonuses even though the company was not performing well. There were too many senior executives who were not doing much except consuming time and space. This is not make-believe. In fact the role was modeled on two real-life people, John and Lewis Gilbert. Everyone in business and everyone who is interested in the stock market should know what they did.

Their Contribution

The Gilbert brothers were born early in the century in very financially comfortable circumstances. They dedicated their lives to having fun, making money, and creating an environment in which companies' boards of directors and senior management were actually accountable to their bosses, the shareholders. They were the original shareholder activists. Among the improvements that they caused or contributed to are the following principles:

- Members of the board of directors should actually own shares of stock in the company.
- Stockholders should receive adequate notice of scheduled annual meetings.
- Stockholders should receive audited financial statements before the annual meeting.
- Annual meetings should be held in a location that is geographically convenient, so that some shareholders can actually attend. An issue in the Transamerica lawsuit, described later, was that the insurance company held its annual meetings in Delaware rather than in California, where its operations and many shareholders were located. The tradition of remote locations for annual meetings has been changed.
- Shareholders can present resolutions for shareholder vote. In 1942, the Securities and Exchange Commission ruled that not only can shareholders present resolutions for a vote, but that their proposals must be circulated to other shareholders at company expense.
- Shareholders can ask questions at annual meetings and actually expect that these questions will be answered. It was common in the 1930s for annual meetings to be filled with company employees who would shout down any stockholder who made an unfavorable comment.
- Senior managers' compensation should be related to the profitability of the company. Putting executive pay in the proxy statement had its effect as early as 1937. The chairman of Bethlehem Steel had to take a pay cut after receiving pressure from the Gilberts. The event received headline coverage from *Business Week* and the *New York Times.*
- Auditors are elected by shareholders, not by management. Auditors should be present at annual meetings to answer shareholders' questions. The concept of internal auditors who would assure the integrity of the company's

financial information was promoted by Lewis Gilbert as early as the 1930s.

- Stockholder proposals are included in proxy statements. In 1945, the Gilbert brothers sued Transamerica Insurance Company because management refused to include in its proxy statement proposals that the Gilberts had made. The judge ruled, "A corporation is run for the benefit of its stockholders and not only for that of its managers." This was a fundamental change in attitude and practice.

These issues seem somewhat obvious in this modern day of shareholder activism and the availability of seemingly unlimited amounts of information through the Internet. When Lewis and John Gilbert hit their full stride in the 1940s, the opposite was true. They are known to have annoyed more than one board chairman with their questions, stockholder resolutions, and challenges.

The Effort Continues

Many years ago, the brothers created a foundation, appropriately called Corporate Democracy, Inc. A team of ten has been organized that travels to many dozens of annual meetings, wherever and whenever they may be held. Meetings that can be reached only after multiple plane rides and car rentals still occasionally occur, but not nearly as frequently as in the past. The team still reports the existence of nonresponsive CEOs. In addition to the activities of this team, Securities and Exchange Commission regulations have increased accountability, and the Internet has vastly expanded the availability of information. However, the effort continues, building momentum for a process that began many years ago.

The most recent improvement in shareholder rights relates to a company's treatment of security analysts, as opposed to those who are "just shareholders." Companies traditionally invited a select few analysts to very comfortable corporate retreats, where management would share its thoughts about the company's past performance and its expectations for the future of the business. This would be followed up with conference calls and other forms of communication with these select few. In fact, these analysts were often made aware of information before it was made available to the general public. They could then advise their clients of critical developments before the general public was aware of them. When a public announcement was finally made, many of these analysts' clients had already traded the stock. To prevent the perception and the fact that the favored few were privy to valuable, otherwise private information, companies are beginning to invite everyone to listen in on their conference calls. Major developments are now often announced to everyone at the same time, either through press releases or through SEC filings. All of this has come about because of the original shareholder activists.

The 10K Report

The 10K is an annual report that goes directly to the Securities and Exchange Commission. It contains all the reports required by regulatory agencies that are contained in the annual report, and more besides. There is no public relations information or photographs. Some 10K reports contain considerable information about the directors and executives, similar to what is given in the proxy statement.

The 10K report of an Internet company that had had a series of particularly disappointing years described the future risks the company faced in continuing in business:

- Uncertainties associated with the company's limited operating history
- Operating losses and the potential need for additional funds
- Unproven acceptance (of the company's products) in a developing market
- Dependence on continuing use of the Internet
- Reliance on advertising revenues and uncertainty concerning the adoption of the Internet as an advertising medium
- Dependence on a limited number of advertisers

- New and highly competitive market; low barriers to entry
- Variations in quarterly results of operations; seasonality
- The need to develop and maintain brand recognition
- Dependence on key personnel and a shortage of qualified information technology (IT) people
- The strain on the company's resources as a result of continued growth
- Inability to identify potential acquisitions and to integrate operations
- Inability to expand and manage international operations
- Dependence on content providers
- Dependence on strategic alliances
- Risk of capacity constraints and systems failures
- Online security risks
- Inability to protect intellectual property
- Liability for informational services
- Government regulation
- Concentration of stock ownership
- Volatility of stock prices
- The antitakeover provisions of Delaware corporate law

The full disclosure provisions of GAAP certainly have caused this company to put its cards on the table. It would be helpful if every company were this honest and forthright in assessing its future. The company also describes in considerable detail how it is coping with each of these risks. It would be valuable to learn what your company and its competitors identify as the risks that might affect its chances of being successful in the future.

The Proxy Statement

The proxy statement is the package of information that each shareholder receives as part of the annual meeting announcement. Because most shareholders do not attend the annual meeting, they are invited to vote by "proxy." This is a mail-in ballot that is essentially the same as an absentee ballot in national elections, with the exception that it also authorizes the person named in the proxy to vote for the shareholder on any

other matter that comes up at the meeting. Shareholders get to
vote for:

- The annual contract with the CPA firm
- Members of the board of directors
- Proposals to change corporate bylaws
- Executive stock option and incentive plans
- Proposals submitted by shareholders

The votes are always yes or no options, and the proxy almost
always indicates the vote that is recommended by the board of
directors. The proxy statement also includes other information
that is of great interest:

1. Notification of the fact that a list of all shareholders is
   available at corporate headquarters and at the annual
   meeting. This is of special interest to shareholder activists
   like the Gilberts who seek to arouse interest in a particular
   issue. It is also valuable to potential acquirers of the company, who need to communicate with shareholders to
   seek support for their efforts.
2. A list of the members of the board of directors, their affil-
   iations, and their compensation. Board members may receive an annual retainer, a fee for each board meeting, a
   fee for each committee meeting, stock options, and deferred compensation. For *Fortune* 500 companies, this
   can amount to $100,000 or more annually.
3. The compensation package for each corporate officer, including deferred compensation and stock options. It is a
   very positive situation if every director and corporate officer has a stake in the success of the company, and if
   their rewards are commensurate with that success, or its
   absence.
4. A description of executive pension and severance pack-
   ages. There has been considerable negative press coverage concerning departed executives who were paid more
   for leaving involuntarily than they were compensated
   when they were employed. The rationale is that their staying with the company would have been more expensive.

Other Sources of Information

There are three ways of obtaining a hard copy of an annual report. The first is from the company itself. The second is through a service provided by a company called Public Register. The Public Register Annual Report Service can be accessed either by telephone or through the company's web site. The service provides the annual reports of thousands of companies. The companies in Public Register's database are organized by industry, so finding the report you want is easy and convenient. The web site is *www.prars.com* and the phone number is 800-4-ANNUAL. Reports are usually received within two business days. This service is free.

The *Wall Street Journal* has a very similar service. The phone number is 800-654-2582. Order forms can also be faxed. It is helpful to get a hard copy of the listing of companies even if you use the *Wall Street Journal* or Public Register Web sites.

The most comprehensive of these services is Morningstar Reports. Morningstar is a Chicago-based organization that is a leading provider of investment information, research, and analysis. It can easily be accessed through America Online. For DuPont and most other companies, this Web site provides:

- A description of the company's businesses
- A listing of its officers
- Three years of financial statements, including the income statement, balance sheet, and statement of cash flows, in considerable detail
- Selected financial ratios segmented by category:
     Financial strength
     Management effectiveness
     Profitability

The management effectiveness ratios include return on equity and return on assets. Profitability ratios include gross profit percentage, operating margin, and return on sales.

The most interesting and helpful section of the report compares the ratios of the subject company with the average ratios for its industry. The DuPont Company is compared with the average of fifty companies classified as "Chemical Manufacturing."

(Recall, however, that DuPont now considers itself a "science" company.) The average performance of all of the Standard & Poor's 500 companies is also listed. The benchmarking value of this information is extraordinary. The ratios are classified into these categories:

- Stock market information, including the price/earnings (P/E) ratio and price/cash flow
- Growth rates of revenues and earnings
- Financial strength
- Profitability
- Management effectiveness
- Efficiency

There are fifty ratios in all. To make the information even more valuable, if that were possible, at the end of the ratios section are the stock symbols of the other forty-nine companies in the chemical database. Each of these other companies can also be accessed.

The Securities and Exchange Commission

The Securities and Exchange Commission (SEC) is a federal government, executive branch agency responsible for assuring fairness in the securities markets. It was formed by the Securities Exchange Act of 1934, known as the "truth in securities" law. This law, together with the Securities Act of 1933 that preceded it, requires public companies to provide investors with financial and other significant information about securities being offered to the public. These laws also prohibit deceit, misrepresentation, and fraud in the sale of securities.

Companies with assets of $10.0 million with securities that are held by more than 500 shareholders are required to file with the SEC. By requiring these companies to register their securities, the SEC provides the public with the information they need if they are to make informed investment decisions. Investors who lose money can recover damages if they can prove that they based their investment decision on information that was misleading, incomplete, or inaccurate. All SEC filings are available on the Internet at the SEC web site, *www.sec.gov.*

SEC rules also govern the solicitation of shareholder votes; proxy statements must be filed with the SEC before the solicitation actually occurs.

Anyone who wishes to make a tender offer for more than 5 percent of a company's stock must also file with the SEC. A tender offer is an offer to purchase shares in large quantities. Tender offers are often announced in the *Wall Street Journal* in an advertisement called a tombstone. Many people or companies that anticipate making an unfriendly tender offer (one that the buyer expects the target company to resist) often purchase 4.99 percent of the stock before the event. Once their holdings exceed 5 percent and their intentions become public, the stock price will move up. Therefore, the buyers will keep their holdings below the threshold until as late in the process as possible in order to keep their intentions secret.

The securities laws also govern the actions of insiders. The term *insider* has two meanings. The legal definition is officers, directors, and anyone who holds more than 5 percent of the stock. These insiders may certainly buy and sell shares, but they must notify the SEC of their transactions. However, anyone who has critical information not available to the general public, far beyond just company management, can also be considered an insider and may not trade the stock on the basis of that information. Morningstar Reports provides information about management purchases and sales of company stock.

The SEC also governs the efforts of SROs, or self-regulated organizations. Included in this classification are the New York and American Stock Exchanges, the National Association of Securities Dealers (NASD), and the regional exchanges. These SROs must create and enforce rules for their members that require them to conform to the SEC regulations and must provide disciplinary proceedings for those whose actions are in violation of these rules but fall short of what is considered criminal. This ensures market integrity and investor protection.

Part 2

ANALYSIS OF FINANCIAL STATEMENTS

Chapter 6

Key Financial Ratios

RATIOS ARE MATHEMATICAL CALCULATIONS THAT the company can use to evaluate its performance. They help the company to determine whether trends are improving or deteriorating. They are calculated by comparing two numbers with each other. The most valuable use that can be made of ratios is to compare the ratios for this year with the same ratios for the previous year and with the ratios of other companies in a similar business. Ratios also serve as goals for future performance.

Statistical Indicators

Many of us use statistical indicators, many of which are actually ratios, to monitor the business. These key indicators include:

- Output per labor hour
- Capacity utilization
- Market share
- Sales orders
- Average length of a production run
- Passenger revenue miles (airlines)
- Responses/mailings (direct mail)

Some of these productivity measures are immediate in nature. They can be monitored on an hourly or daily basis, and management can make immediate adjustments in response to them. These are very much "real-time" indicators.

These statistical indicators are very much the domain of internal management. While internal statistical information would certainly be interesting and might be valuable to outsiders, they have little or no access to it. Interestingly, in the automobile business, information concerning units produced, units sold, and available inventory are public information. But this is an exception.

First-level line managers in both sales and operations require detailed statistical information on a regular basis—and frequently. Operations supervisors fine-tune machinery, redeploy labor resources, and manage the logistics of inventory. Sales managers direct daily or weekly sales calls, schedule appearances at trade shows, and determine immediate customer satisfaction. Senior managers don't require this degree of detail to carry out their responsibilities, and certainly not on an hourly, daily, or even weekly basis. The higher the manager's level of responsibility, the more an overview is the necessary perspective. That explains why, as managers progress through the organization's ranks, their concerns and perspectives become more financial and strategic.

Financial Ratios

Financial ratios provide more of an overview. They help management to monitor the company's performance over a period of time, perhaps a week or a month. In order to fully appreciate and properly use the financial ratios, it is important that the analyst:

- Understand the business and its products
- Analyze the company's performance within the context of the economic climate
- Be aware of the legal and regulatory issues that the company faces
- Look at the ratios within the context of the competitive environment

- Be knowledgeable about industry averages and ratio behavior

People with a wide variety of interests may use financial ratios to analyze the business. These include:

External

- Security analysts
- Potential and existing stockholders
- Bankers and other lenders
- Suppliers and their credit managers
- Competitors
- Regulators

Internal

- Board of directors
- Senior management
- Operations, sales, finance, human resources, marketing
- Strategic planners

Each of these groups has its own perspectives and needs. Developing a marketing strategy requires an understanding of the company's financial ability to support growth. Suppliers assess the company's ability (not its willingness) to pay its bills in accordance with agreed-upon credit terms

Ratios must be evaluated within their context. The value of statistical indicators has been discussed. Many business and environmental factors have been identified. As mentioned previously, the most valuable use that can be made of ratios is to look at them as part of a trend and to compare them with the same ratios for competitors.

Financial ratios can be divided into four major groupings:

1. Liquidity ratios
2. Working capital management ratios
3. Measures of profitability
4. Financial leverage ratios

There are many different ratios, and their exact definitions vary. What follows is an extensive description of the key ratios, presented with very workable definitions.

Liquidity Ratios

Liquidity measures are used to evaluate a company's ability to pay its bills on a regular week-to-week or month-to-month basis. There are two commonly used ratios that help to evaluate this, the current ratio and the quick ratio.

Current Ratio

The current ratio compares *current assets* with *current liabilities.* The specific ratio is:

$$\frac{\text{Cash} + \text{Marketable Securities} + \text{Accounts Receivable} + \text{Inventory} + \text{Other Current Assets}}{\text{Accounts Payable} + \text{Bank (Short-Term) Debt} + \text{Accrued Liabilities} + \text{Other Current Liabilities}} = \text{Current Ratio}$$

A ratio below 1.0 means that current assets are less than current liabilities. This is a clear indication that the company has liquidity problems. However, a ratio in excess of 1.0 does not necessarily mean that the company is adequately liquid. Higher is not necessarily better. The ratio can be high because the company has too much inventory or does a poor job of collecting its accounts receivable in a timely manner. Conversely, the ratio can be low because the company does not have or cannot afford the levels of inventory necessary to serve its customers in a competitive manner. Too much working capital is poor asset management; it is very expensive, can restrict cash flow, and inhibits the company's ability to grow and prosper.

An appropriate ratio can be intelligently developed by evaluating each individual component. The questions to be answered include: How much cash and near cash does the company need in order to pay its bills and manage its very short-term liquidity? What credit terms should the company offer its customers as part of its strategy to satisfy those customers? What levels of finished goods inventory are needed to serve the marketplace? How much raw materials and components inventory is required to assure efficient production operations? These and other questions need to be answered in order to determine the current ratio that the company should try to achieve. Usually a "range of desirability" is created to adjust for seasonality and peak periods. So, an example of the target ratio to assure intelligent asset management might be 1.8 to 2.2.

Metropolitan Manufacturing Company Current Ratio

	2002	2001
Current Assets	$2,009,000	$1,645,000
Current Liabilities	$898,000	$619,000
Current Ratio	2.23	2.65

Metropolitan's current ratio has declined somewhat, although all of the absolute amounts have increased significantly. Bank debt and accounts payable have increased, primarily to finance the much higher levels of inventory. As long as the interest on the bank debt and the conditions or restrictions imposed by the loan are not too burdensome, there does not appear to be a problem. The ratio itself remains at a reasonable level, especially for a manufacturing company.

Quick Ratio ("Acid Test" Ratio)

The quick ratio has the same purpose as the current ratio, but it is more immediate. It is the same as the current ratio except that it does not include inventory. Therefore, the ratio is:

$$\frac{\text{Cash} +}{\begin{array}{c}\text{Marketable Securities} + \\ \text{Accounts Receivable}\end{array}} = \text{Quick Ratio}$$
$$\frac{}{\begin{array}{c}\text{Accounts Payable} + \\ \text{Bank (Short-Term) Debt} + \\ \text{Accrued Liabilities} + \\ \text{Other Current Liabilities}\end{array}}$$

In order to use the quick ratio as an analytical tool, it must be understood that there is a great difference in liquidity between accounts receivable and inventory. When a company is owed money by its customers (accounts receivable), it has already done its work; it has fulfilled its commitment by delivering fine products and services. Whatever money was necessary to accomplish this has already been spent. However—and it is a big however—in order to "liquefy" its inventory, the company must spend additional funds. Raw materials and work-in-process inventory have not yet become finished products. There is still work to be done, and funds still must be spent. While finished goods inventory has been completed, it has not yet been sold and delivered. Therefore, inventory is not a very liquid asset. It is classified as a current asset because it is expected to be turned into cash in less than a year, possibly within six months or even two months. Thus, it is a liquid asset when compared to fixed assets and long-term investments, but it is not liquid in the way that marketable securities and accounts receivable are.

Given all of this, a quick ratio in the vicinity of 0.8 is probably acceptable. Because a service business has no or little inventory, its current and quick ratios will be the same number.

Metropolitan Manufacturing Company Quick Ratio:

"Quick" Assets	$780,000	$714,000
Liabilities	$898,000	$619,000
	0.87	1.15

Metropolitan's quick ratio has declined from a level that is extremely comfortable to one that is merely comfortable. This presumes, of course, that the terms of the bank debt are not onerous and that the company's very heavy investment in inventory proves to be profitable. We will examine these issues further when we analyze working capital management.

Exceptions to Comfortable Levels

There are exceptions to our prior statement concerning comfortable levels for these liquidity ratios. If the current and quick ratios were in the "comfortable" range, but a substantial amount of bank debt were due the next day, the future of the company could be in serious jeopardy. If the current ratio were in the comfortable range, but the finished goods inventory that the company had on hand was not what the customers wanted, then the company's ability to deliver product to its customers in a timely manner would be impaired, even though its current ratio was acceptable.

Working Capital Management Ratios

These ratios and measures assist a company in evaluating its performance regarding the management of the credit function, as reflected in accounts receivable, and also the management of inventory.

Days' Sales Outstanding

Days' sales outstanding measures the average number of days that the company is taking to collect accounts receivable from its customers. The formula is:

$$\frac{\text{Annual Revenue}}{365} = \frac{\text{Accounts Receivable}}{\text{Average Revenue per Day}} = \frac{\text{Days' Sales}}{\text{Outstanding}}$$

When a company extends credit, it gives its customers the opportunity to pay the company later rather than paying upon receipt of the company's products or services. Credit terms are provided because giving credit helps to sell product. Extending credit gives the company a competitive advantage (and not doing so would probably put it at a competitive disadvantage).

If average days' sales outstanding is 43 days, that means that, on average, it is taking that many days to collect owed funds from the customer, from the date of the invoice to the date when the funds are collected. This should be measured against the credit terms of sale. If credit terms are 30 days, a collection period of 40 to 42 days should be perceived as acceptable. Cash sales, if any, should be excluded from the calculation.

Metropolitan Manufacturing Company Days' Sales Outstanding 2002:

$$\frac{4,160,000}{365} = \$11,397 \qquad \frac{637,000}{11,397} = 56 \text{ days}$$

2001:

$$\frac{3,900,000}{365} = \$10,685 \qquad \frac{597,000}{10,685} = 56 \text{ days}$$

Assuming that Metropolitan's credit terms are 30 days, the company's accounts receivable are too high. The salespeople probably are not communicating the terms of sale clearly, if they are communicating them at all, and collection procedures overall need to be improved. The company can add a "free" $11,397 to its bank account for each day that average days' sales outstanding is reduced. To analyze the receivables management further, and to ensure that this conclusion is not distorted by statistical or seasonal aberration, the finance manager should also prepare an aging of accounts receivable.

Aging of Accounts Receivables

An aging of accounts receivable is a detailed listing of how long the company has been waiting for its customers to pay their bills. Generally, much of the accounts receivable balance will not yet be due, as the amounts will have been billed less than 30 days earlier. A considerable sum might be more than 30 but less than 45 days old, or less than 15 days overdue. The existence of bills more than 45 days old is a sure indicator of customers' inability or unwillingness to pay or of a feeling on the part of customers that there is no particular pressure to do so.

The aging for Metropolitan Manufacturing Company as of December 31, 2002, is:

Less than 30 days	$280,000
30–45 days	196,000
45–60 days	135,000
Above 60 days	36,000
Total	$647,000

Metropolitan Manufacturing Company clearly has some problem receivables. The probability that the company will be able to collect those that are over 60 days old is not good. The collections people in the accounting department clearly have challenges ahead if they are to get that money. The desirability of continuing to do business with those customers should be evaluated. Those customers whose receivables are in the 45- to 60-day range should receive some attention before they too become a worsening problem. Clearly, Metropolitan Manufacturing must change its attitude and those of its customers and begin to change some of its philosophies and practices.

Receivables Management Can Be Improved

Reducing accounts receivable without jeopardizing sales volume is a very effective way for your company to improve its cash flow. The following list gives basic concepts of credit management that you should consider when you are negotiating with existing and potential customers. Not every idea will work in all situations, and some of these ideas may not be appropriate for your business at all. However, nothing will work if you don't try it.

1. *Be aware that credit is a sales tool.* Credit is granted to customers (permitting them to defer payment on merchandise that they already possess and are benefiting from) in order to motivate them to buy and in order to provide an additional competitive advantage. Put credit

extension to the test: Will it affect whether or not the customer buys from you? Will it motivate the customer to buy more or buy again? You are entitled to your money. You have earned it; you have spent money to make the sale, and you have provided the customer with the finest product or service of its kind.

2. *Never make the extension of credit automatic.* Train your sales, service, and delivery people to reinforce your credit strategies.

3. *Cheerfully extend credit if the customer asks for it and deserves it.* Ask the customer how much time he would like to have. Never extend credit for an automatic 30 or 60 days. Some customers will ask for less credit than you would otherwise have granted. Customers will pay faster in order to maintain credibility with a very important supplier.

4. *Train your customers to pay fast.* Understanding that old habits die slowly, let the quality of your products and services, rather than your willingness to be a banker, be their motive for buying from you.

5. *Get the clock ticking.* Agreed-upon credit terms should start the day the product is delivered, not the day the invoice is mailed. Mail out invoices and statements more frequently. This is effective and is rarely noticed. Give the customer the invoice upon delivery, if possible. This reduces mailing expenses and makes the customer even more conscious of the responsibility to pay you fast.

6. *Never apologize for asking for your money.* You earned it by providing the finest products and services in your marketplace.

7. *Search for opportunities to reduce your outstanding receivables.* Start slowly, with your new customers and your least desirable existing customers. Train them and those who work for you. Set yourself a six-month target and work toward it. Watch your bank account grow.

Inventory Turnover Ratio

The inventory turnover ratio provides a helpful overview of how effectively the company manages what may be its most valuable asset, its inventory. It describes the relationship between the cost of the product sold over the course of a year and the average inventory the company maintained to support those sales. The formula for the inventory turnover ratio is:

$$\frac{\text{Cost of Goods Sold}}{\text{Average Inventory}} = \text{Inventory Turnover}$$

The resulting inventory turnover is interpreted as follows:

- A turnover of 12 times translates to one month's inventory on hand, on average.
- A turnover of 25 times translates to two weeks' inventory on hand, on average.
- A turnover of 6 times translates to two months' inventory on hand, on average.

Of course, determining the appropriate amount of inventory for a company is much more complex than calculating this ratio, however valuable the ratio may be.

The cost of inventory includes the following:

- Acquisition cost
- Transportation in and out
- Insurance
- Personal property taxes
- Warehouse overhead
- Labor expense
- Computer and related expenses
- Interest expense
- Physical deterioration
- Seasonal obsolescence

The cost of not having enough inventory or of having the wrong inventory includes:

- Unhappy customers
- Lost market share

- Higher production costs in the form of overtime or extra shifts
- Purchasing small quantities at short notice
- Paying extra for accelerated transportation

Finished Goods Inventory. *Efficiency of Production.* The more efficient the production operations are, the less finished product a company must maintain. If operations are inefficient, the company will have to have a safety stock of finished product to assure adequate customer service.

Made to Order/Made for Stock. A company that makes product without an order in hand will have to maintain extra inventory because of the uncertainty associated with what products customers will demand. A company that makes product in response to specific orders, especially custom-designed product, will require very little or no inventory on hand other than the inventory that is being accumulated for shipment.

Forecasting Sales. The more effectively a company can predict what its customers will want, the less finished product inventory it will require. If there is great uncertainty concerning the customers' needs and/or the directions that the markets will take, the company will have to keep more product on hand to assure customer service.

Lead Times. The more notice that the customers give the company concerning their product requirements, the less extra inventory the company must maintain.

Low-value-added distributors must have adequate supplies of almost everything on hand in order to serve their customers and be competitive. In fact, their *value added* is precisely their having everything on hand, ready for immediate delivery or pickup. The ultimate low-value-added business is a supermarket. It changes the nature or content of the product very little; all it does is take crates of twelve or more items, open them, and put the contents on convenient shelves. Its value added is having 35,000 of these products in one large, clean, comfortable room.

And, a supermarket cannot run out of any essential items and hope to keep its customers happy.

Number of Warehouse Locations. Some companies serve their entire marketplace from a single warehouse. This is efficient if the marketplace is geographically concentrated and can be properly served from that one location. It can be effective even if the marketplace is national in scope if the product is very valuable or orders are very large, making transportation a small part of the total cost. It can also be effective if deliveries are not too time-sensitive, so that surface or ocean transportation can be used.

However, in the absence of any of these conditions, many businesses must use a network of warehouses, and perhaps even satellites of those warehouses, to serve their customers. If a company has warehouses at multiple locations, inventory levels relative to volumes sold will be higher than those of a business with a single warehouse. Safety stocks will also be higher to protect against transportation uncertainties. Minimum stocks of each product line must be stored in order to assure customer service. The offset to these higher costs and inventory levels should be more timely customer service and more efficient transportation, with products being transported in bulk over the long distances from the factory to each warehouse rather than being transported individually over the long distances from the central warehouse to each customer. A financial analysis of these alternatives should be provided to assure cost efficiency.

Raw Materials/Purchased Components. *Product Diversity.* The greater the variety of products that a company manufactures, the greater the amount of raw materials and components that it must keep on hand. For each type of product, the company needs to have a minimum stock of materials and components on hand. This is especially true when the company's finished products have few if any components in common. Commonality of components contributes considerably to the minimization of inventory. An excellent example of this is the automobile industry. Many different models of cars actually have many components, including the frames, in common. In fact, there are many different models of cars that are actually the same car, despite different appearances and perceptions of quality.

Supply Chain Management. Technology has had a dramatic impact on inventory management and has resulted in drastic re-ductions in all forms of inventory. When a company goes online with its vendors, its product needs are automatically communi-cated to those vendors electronically. This shortens lead times, reduces mistakes, and accelerates the supply process. Greater competitive intensity forces suppliers to provide faster delivery of high-quality products. Safety stock can be reduced when quality problems are reduced.

Concentration/Diversity of Vendors. Technology, especially the business-to-business (B2B) capabilities of the Internet, has created both incredible supply chain turmoil and incredible op-portunity at the same time. Internet hookups between vendor and customer give that vendor a considerable competitive ad-vantage, assuming that the vendor's performance remains at the highest quality levels. On the other hand, product web sites and transportation logistics have created a nationwide supply mar-ket. Companies used to buy product from relatively local ven-dors. Now they can access the Internet and locate suppliers all over the country. The intensity of the resulting competition, along with very dependable transportation support from compa-nies like Federal Express and UPS, leads to lower purchase costs, shorter lead times, and less inventory.

Metropolitan Manufacturing Company Inventory Turnover

	2002	2001	
Cost of Goods Sold	$2,759,000	$2,593,000	(line 25)
Ending Inventory*	$1,229,000	$931,000	(line 4)
Inventory Turnover	2.24 times	2.79 times	

*In general, the inventory figure used is the average of the beginning and ending inventories. In this example, for simplicity, I have used ending inventory.

The inventory turnover ratio for Metropolitan Manufacturing Company is quite low. This could be because Metropolitan's business is very inventory-intensive. Perhaps Metropolitan is a very vertically integrated manufacturing company. Or perhaps Metropolitan is in a service-intensive business with short lead times, resulting in a need for vast quantities of finished goods inventory. Or the company could be purchasing raw materials inventory in large quantities in order to take advantage of quantity discounts. If this last alternative is true, Metropolitan's gross profit margin should be considerably above the average for its industry. Alternatively, the high levels of inventory could be the result of gross inefficiencies, ineffective purchasing, and overly optimistic sales forecasts that are not being achieved. Knowledge of Metropolitan's industry, its operations plan, and its competitors would be very valuable in reaching an accurate conclusion.

Measures of Profitability

These ratios assist management and others in the evaluation of the company's achievements. They focus on:

- Profitability achieved by the management team
- Assets invested in the business
- Revenue achieved by the business
- The funds that the owners have invested in the business

Some review of terms will be helpful. The line numbers used here and later in the chapter refer to the financial statements in Chapters 1 and 2 (Exhibits 1-1 and 2-1).

24.	Revenue: The value of products and services sold.
25.	Cost of goods sold: The cost of the labor, materials, and manufacturing overhead used to produce the products sold.
26.	Gross profit: Revenue − cost of goods sold (same as gross margin).
27.	General and administrative expenses: The cost of operating the company itself; this category includes all other support spending necessary to conduct the business.

27a. Earnings before interest, taxes, and depreciation and amortization: This is known by its acronym, EBITDA.
28. Depreciation (and other noncash) expense.
29. Net income before taxes.
30. Provision for income taxes.
31. Net income.

Our analysis of these numbers would be improved if we knew more about Metropolitan Manufacturing Company, including:

- Its business and products
- The competitive environment
- Its degree of globalization
- The budget for year 2002 and its plans for subsequent years
- Legal and regulatory issues
- Whether it is a public or a private organization
- Its capacity utilization
- Its fixed cost/variable cost mix

The selection of the numbers to use in the analysis depends upon:

- What is being measured
- Who is doing the analysis
- Which managers are being measured
- Style and measurement attitude

Issues of Selecting Measurements

The board of directors of the company, as well as security analysts and credit analysts, is concerned with the performance of the company as a whole. Therefore, the measure they use to evaluate company-wide performance will probably be *net income*. Increasingly, however, security analysts, who are concerned with the company's performance within the context of the stock market, are using EBITDA.

Many people consider the provision for income taxes to be a passive expense. To begin with, the amount of federal income taxes shown on the financial statements is not the actual amount that the company paid. It is essentially the corporate tax rate, currently 34 percent, multiplied by the amount of net income before tax. As a result, many analysts use the pretax amount to measure profitability.

Analysts are often very concerned with and focus on the operating cash flow that was generated by the business. To look at this, they often use EBITDA. In addition, EBITDA is often used to evaluate the performance of those who manage individual businesses, strategic business units, and individual divisions and subsidiaries. The rationale is that the managers of these entities are not responsible for, and therefore need not be concerned with, taxes and the income and expenses associated with the financing of the corporation, i.e., interest income and interest expense. They are evaluated on those results for which they are responsible, which leads to a focus on the generation of operational cash flow. Hence, EBITDA is used.

To measure the performance of an individual product, gross profit should be used. The resulting ratio is the gross profit percentage, calculated as follows:

$$\frac{\text{Gross Profit}}{\text{Revenue}} = \text{Gross Profit Percentage}$$

	2002	2001	
Gross Profit	$1,401	$1,307	(line 26)
Revenue	$4,160	$3,900	(line 24)
Gross Profit Percentage	34%	34%	

It should be noted that in this discussion, gross profit and gross margin are considered to be synonymous terms and are used interchangeably. Some companies differentiate the two.

A gross margin of 34 percent is a considerable achievement for a manufacturing company. This suggests that the company is providing some value added through its business. A warehouse distributor might have gross margins in the 20 to 25 percent range, while manufacturers of high-end medical products and pharmaceuticals might enjoy margins of as much as 60 to 70 percent on some of their products. We should note, however, that despite an additional investment in inventory of $298,000 in 2002, Metropolitan's gross margin did not improve.

Return on assets (ROA) measures the profitability of the company relative to the total amount of assets the owners have invested in the business. These assets include both working capital (cash, marketable securities, accounts receivable, and inventory) and fixed assets (capital equipment and land/buildings). The equation for return on assets is:

$$\frac{\text{Net Income}}{\text{Assets}} = \text{Return on Assets}$$

In addition to measuring the overall performance of the company, return on equity (ROE) measures the company's ability to use borrowed funds effectively as well as the owners' money. This will also affect the company's ability to attract new investors. Without debt, a company's ROA and ROE will be the same. The more debt is used to expand the business, the greater will be the improvement in return on equity compared with return on assets. However, excessive reliance on borrowed funds involves considerable risk, as we will see later when we discuss financial leverage. The formula for return on equity is:

$$\frac{\text{Net Income}}{\text{Stockholders' Equity}} = \text{Return on Equity}$$

Return on sales measures the overall operating efficiency of the company. Among the questions that it answers are: Is the production facility operating effectively? Are the administrative departments performing their responsibilities efficiently? The equation is:

$$\frac{\text{Net Income}}{\text{Revenue}} = \text{Return on Sales}$$

Metropolitan Manufacturing Company Operating Performance

Return on Assets:

		2002	2001
$\dfrac{\text{Net Income}}{\text{Assets}}$	$=$	$\dfrac{\$156,000}{\$3,202,000^*}$	$\dfrac{\$190,000}{\$2,863,000^*}$

*Year-end amounts are used.

	2002	2001
ROA	4.9%	6.6%

We can readily observe that not only has Metropolitan's net income actually declined, but its ROA has declined even more as a result of the increase in the company's asset base.

Return on Equity

		2002	2001
$\dfrac{\text{Net Income}}{\text{Stockholders' Equity}}$	$=$	$\dfrac{\$156,000}{\$2,004,000}$	$\dfrac{\$190,000}{\$1,894,000}$

	2002	2001
ROE	7.8%	10.0%

Metropolitan's ROE has also declined. Notice that the company's ROE is greater than its ROA because of its use of financial leverage (borrowed funds). This calculation, for simplicity, uses end-of-year balances. We also used this for the ROA calculation. Either is correct and accurate as long as the numbers used are consistent from year to year.

Metropolitan is reinvesting a considerable portion of its profits in the business rather than distributing most of the profits to its owners in the form of dividends, as can be seen from the substantial increase in the retained earnings number (line 21) on the balance sheet. This is a very positive sign. Also, line 33 on the income statement tells us exactly how much of the profits were reinvested in the business. In 2002, this amount was $110,000 out of a total net income of $156,000. The difference is explained by a cash dividend payment of $46,000.

Management/owners reinvesting a sizable portion of the

company's net income in the business is a very positive sign because it demonstrates their confidence in the business. It also
indicates that while the owners recognize the need to modernize
and expand the company, they do not want to rely too heavily on
debt to finance the company's growth. Instead, they are willing
to use reinvested profits as part of the financing. Unfortunately,
one short-term result of this decision may be, as happened here,
a decline in ROE, and this can be perceived as negative. Had the
net income stayed flat at $190,000 rather than declining, ROE
would still have gone down, although not by as much as it in fact
did. Therefore, companies face the dilemma of sometimes having to choose between the long-term benefits of expansion and
modernization or favorable short-term results. Metropolitan's
owners were willing to take the longer-term view. If this were a
public company, they would have to explain their decision to the
Wall Street crowd.

Return on Sales

		2002	2001	
$\dfrac{\text{Net Income}}{\text{Revenue}}$	=	$156,000	$190,000	(line 31)
		$4,160,000	$3,900,000	(line 24)
		3.75%	4.9%	

Metropolitan's financial ratios clearly indicate declining performance. There are several possible explanations:

- Intense competition, causing pricing pressure and declin-
  ing margins
- Operational inefficiency
- Spending to prepare for future strategic moves

If reduced prices and/or volume were the cause of the decline in
the ratios, we would normally have expected gross margins to
decline. However, the gross profit margin did not decline, but
remained constant at 34 percent. This could still be the explanation if the company was able to reduce its manufacturing costs
commensurately, as evidenced by lower cost of goods sold.

Quantity discounts stemming from larger-quantity purchases of raw materials and purchased components could have contributed to maintenance of the margins. This probably did happen, since inventory levels were much higher and inventory turnover was lower. So perhaps the company protected its 34 percent gross margin through inventory purchases. While we consider these issues, let's not lose sight of the fact that revenue did increase between 2001 and 2002 by more than 6 percent (line 24). It would be very helpful if we knew whether the increase in revenue was explained by price changes, volume changes, mix changes, new products, or a combination of these. This is critical information that typical financial reports may not provide, but should.

Notice that annual depreciation expense increased only slightly between 2002 and 2001 (line 28), even though the company made capital expenditures amounting to $34,000 (line 41). This suggests that the capital expenditures probably involved replacement of assets rather than expansion. If there had been an expansion, annual depreciation expenses would have increased.

General and administrative expenses increased appreciably between 2001 and 2002 (line 27). The backup detail would tell us whether this spending was an investment in the company's future, such as expanding the sales organization or increasing spending on research, or whether it was additional spending on important, but less critical, added staff.

Financial Leverage Ratios

Borrowing funds to finance expansion or modernization is a very positive strategy if the terms of the loan are not too burdensome. We certainly don't want the interest rate to be too high. Perhaps more important, we want the benefits of the investments to be achieved before the debt becomes due. Many companies have experienced financial problems because their bank debts came due before their investment projects achieved their forecasted benefits. In such cases, when the loans come due, the company has yet to generate the cash flow needed to repay them and as a result finds itself in a very uncomfortable position. Often the term of the loan is more critical than the actual interest rate paid.

If a company can achieve an after-tax return on investment of 25 percent on a project that will reach fruition in three years, whether the cost of the money needed for that project is 9.0 percent or 9.5 percent is not going to change the decision to invest in the project as long as the loan has a maturity of more than three years. If the financing is a one-year bank loan, the company will not have the cash to repay it and may be forced to cut back the project and reduce expenses at exactly the wrong time (if it is unable to refinance the loan). So, while the cost of funds is important, you should focus on the repayment schedule, as well.

Debt/Equity Ratio

The debt/equity ratio measures risk from the perspective of both the company and existing and potential lenders. The primary risk to the company is that both principal and interest payments on debt are fixed costs. They must be paid even if the company's business and its cash flow decline. The other risk to the company is that if its ratios decline, it may violate its loan agreements. This might trigger higher interest rates or, worse, calling of the loan.

$$\frac{\text{Long-Term Debt}}{\text{Stockholders' Equity}} = \text{Debt/Equity Ratio}$$

Short-term bank debt is also a source of risk. Repayment of this debt is also a fixed cost, and its due date is more immediate than that of long-term debt. Remember that short-term debt is due in less than one year. Some analysts redefine the debt/equity ratio to include bank debt, as follows:

$$\frac{\text{Bank Debt} + \text{Long-Term Debt}}{\text{Stockholders' Equity}} = \frac{\text{Funded Debt}}{\text{Stockholders' Equity}}$$

Funded debt refers to funds of all maturities borrowed from financial institutions. For most manufacturing companies, a debt/equity ratio of more than 0.5 is perceived to be on the borderline of being risky. This would not be true if the company were a public utility or a very high-quality commercial real estate company. For manufacturing or service businesses, a funded debt/

equity ratio in excess of 0.6 or 0.7 to 1 is interpreted as definitely approaching the risky stage.

Interest Coverage

This describes the cushion that the company has between the amount of cash it generates before interest expense and taxes and the amount of interest it must pay on its debt. This margin of safety is usually prescribed by the lending institutions as a condition of making the loan. The desired coverage ratio is based upon:

- The quality of the assets used as collateral, if any
- The profitability history of the company
- The predictability of the company's earnings

The greater the predictability and certainty of the company's earnings and the higher its growth, the lower the required interest coverage ratio will be. The figure used to measure the amount of cash available to pay interest expense is EBITDA.

$$\frac{\text{EBITDA}}{\text{Interest Expense}} = \text{Interest Coverage}$$

Sometimes the company is required to make regular payments of principal along with the interest. The payment of principal plus interest is called *debt service*. Such payments are exactly the same as the monthly payments that individuals make to the bank on a home mortgage, which include principal as well as interest. When a company is required to do this, some analysts and financial institutions will calculate the coverage ratio to include the principal payments with the interest. This is called *debt service coverage*. Still another version of this ratio also includes lease payments on the premise that long-term leases are in fact a form of equipment financing. All of these versions are valid and helpful. Using the same version consistently once the methodology has been selected is important.

Metropolitan Manufacturing Company Financial Leverage Ratios

Debt/Equity:

	2002	2001	
$\dfrac{\text{Long-Term Debt}}{\text{Stockholders' Equity}} =$	$300,000	$350,000	(line 17)
	$2,004,000	$1,894,000	(line 22)
Debt/Equity Ratio	15%	18.5%	

Metropolitan's debt/equity ratio is very low. A ratio below 50 percent would probably be perceived as comfortable. Also, notice that Metropolitan paid off $50,000 in long-term debt. We know that this was voluntary because, by definition, long-term debt is not due in the upcoming year. Not only is low debt a favorable condition from a risk perspective, but the lenders will look upon reinvested net income as a very positive event. Metropolitan's interest rate is probably not too high.

Interest Coverage:

$$\frac{\text{EBITDA (line 27a)}}{\text{Interest Expense}} = \frac{\$368,000}{\$48,000 \; [8\% \times (\$300,000 + \$300,000)]}$$
$$= 7.7 \text{ times}$$

Interest coverage of 4 to 5 times is considered acceptable. A coverage ratio of 7.7 times is well within the comfort level. When this is combined with a debt/equity ratio of 15 percent, it appears that Metropolitan Manufacturing is not at all at risk. It certainly has the capacity to borrow more funds.

Debt/Equity Ratio and Return on Equity

Exhibit 6-1 clearly demonstrates the risks and rewards that companies experience as they increase their levels of debt. The reward is an improved return on equity. The risk is higher interest expense and debt service requirements that become increasingly difficult to meet.

Using earnings before interest and taxes (EBIT), this company is achieving a return on assets of 20 percent, as follows:

Exhibit 6-1.

	EBIT	Assets	Debt/Equity	ROE	Interest Coverage
1.	$200,000	$1,000,000	0	10%	—
2.	$200,000	$1,000,000	100/900	11%	20.0 times
3.	$200,000	$1,000,000	300/700	12%	6.7
4.	$200,000	$1,000,000	500/500	15%	4.0
5.	$200,000	$1,000,000	700/300	22%	2.9
6.	$200,000	$1,000,000	900/100	55%	2.2

$$\frac{EBIT}{Assets} = \frac{\$200,000}{\$1,000,000}$$

To simplify the example, we will make the following assumptions:

The interest rate is 10 percent.
The tax rate is 50 percent.

The *Return on Equity* calculation is:

$$\frac{(EBIT - Interest)/2 = Net\ Income}{Stockholders'\ Equity}$$

1. $\dfrac{(\$200,000 - 0) = \$200,000}{\$1,000,000} = 20\%$

2. $\dfrac{(\$200,000 - 10,000)/2 = \$95,000}{\$900,000} = 11\%$

3. $\dfrac{(\$200,000 - 30,000)/2 = \$85,000}{\$700,000} = 12\%$

6. $\dfrac{(\$200,000 - 90,000)/2 = \$55,000}{\$100,000} = 55\%$

The *Interest Coverage Ratio* is:

EBIT/Interest Expense

$200,000/$10,000
= 20.0 times

$200,000/$30,000
= 6.7 times

$200,000/$90,000
= 2.2 times

For a given level of earnings before interest and taxes, the more debt the company takes on in its capitalization structure, the greater the return on equity will be. However, the higher the debt/equity ratio, the greater the possibility that a downturn in earnings will leave the company unable to meet its interest payment obligations. If a company with the structure shown in line 1 has a severe earnings downturn, this will cause extreme unhappiness among management (and probably shareholders). But the company will still continue in business. If a company with the structure shown in line 6 experiences a similar downturn, it will probably be in default on its loans.

Companies with very predictable, high-quality earnings can afford a high debt/equity ratio, especially if they have considerable fixed assets to provide collateral for the loans. Economic conditions and current events aside, examples are commercial real estate and power utilities. Start-up and Internet companies generally have no earnings at all, or at best very erratic earnings. They generally do not qualify for loans from financial institutions.

Chapter 7

Using Return on Assets to Measure Profit Centers

THE USE OF RETURN ON assets is extremely valuable in the management of profit centers. A profit center is a business entity that is dedicated to a specific market, distribution channel, or set of customers. It has its own strategy and perhaps even its own business model, the model best suited to making that type of business successful and profitable. These profit centers may be called strategic business units (SBUs). Each profit center has its own balance sheet, for which the unit's management is responsible.

These businesses need not be legal entities, nor do they need to have complete balance sheet responsibility. In many cases, SBUs are responsible only for the asset side of the balance sheet. The corporate parent remains responsible for the liabilities and any stockholder issues. The SBU's mandate is to achieve a profit and to use the assets for which it is responsible with maximum effectiveness.

The return on assets analytical model that we are going to use is called the DuPont formula. Its roots can be traced back at least 75 years, but its age does not diminish its value. In fact, its durability says much for its usefulness. The formula can be found in the archives of the DuPont Chemical Company. Like most analytical techniques, it was probably an adaptation of other formulas that existed before its time. Nothing is totally new.

Techniques and formulas evolve and are adapted over time to take advantage of newer ideas and business developments. The formula is:

$$\text{ROA} = \underset{\underset{\textbf{(3)}}{\text{Revenue}}}{\overset{\overset{\textbf{(4)}}{\text{After-Tax Cash Flow (ATCF)}}}{}} \times \underset{\underset{\textbf{(1)}}{\text{Assets}}}{\overset{\overset{\textbf{(2)}}{\text{Revenue}}}{}} = \underset{\underset{\textbf{(6)}}{\text{Assets}}}{\overset{\overset{\textbf{(5)}}{\text{ATCF}}}{}}$$

1 and 6. Assets

The profitability of any business is certainly affected by the amount of assets that are dedicated to that business. These assets include cash, accounts receivable, inventory, and fixed assets.

Cash

The size of the working cash balances needed by the business depends on its managers' overall ability to predict and manage cash inflows and outflows. In some larger companies, the profit centers do not manage their cash balances at all. Instead, these balances are consolidated at the corporate level to provide a maximum return on the cash invested.

Accounts Receivable

What are the credit terms that the SBU offers when it sells its products or services to its customers? The answer to this question depends on the type of business the SBU is in and the competitive environment. The accounts receivable on the SBU's books will also be affected by how well the SBU communicates these credit terms to its customers and how effectively it enforces those policies.

Inventory

There are a multitude of issues that affect this investment, including supply chain management, how vertically integrated the operation is, and how efficiently the operation is run.

The degree of vertical integration refers to how much of the overall production process is done by the company itself rather than being outsourced. The more vertically integrated the business is, the greater the amount of the value-adding process that is performed by the company. A vertically integrated oil company drills for the petroleum, owns and operates the refineries, stores the finished product, and has a major chain of retail gas stations on our nation's highways. In contrast, there are companies that only own and operate retail gas stations; such a company purchases the gasoline it sells from outside sources—perhaps from distributors, but often from the fully integrated oil companies. (Yes, they may buy from their competitors.) Generally, with some exceptions, the more vertically integrated the company's operations, the more inventory investment it will have for longer periods of time.

Fixed Assets

The previous discussion of vertical integration also applies to the business's investment in fixed assets. A company that is vertically integrated requires a tremendous investment in fixed assets and incurs significant expense for maintaining them.

The type of business the company is in and how it chooses to conduct that business will also greatly affect its investment in fixed assets. A three shift operation requires less equipment than a two- or one-shift operation producing the same amount. The question, then, is: Why would a company run a one-shift operation, which requires so much extra equipment, when it can operate with less equipment on a three-shift basis? The answer is that it would not unless there were other factors involved.

A three-shift operation is most applicable to a machine-driven mass-production operation where the products are the same or similar and value-added labor input is not that critical. Examples are chemical, steel, and paper companies. A business that requires very highly skilled labor or that requires extensive supervision may be most profitable in a one-shift operation. There may not be enough high-quality labor or supervision available to operate around the clock. Custom-designed products require considerable management attention. Also, the businesses in which around-the-clock operations are desirable are often those in which it is prohibitively expensive to stop the machines, and so they must run continuously. A steel furnace cannot be economically shut down at 5 P.M. and restarted the next morning. If a chemical plant were shut down, it would take weeks to clean up the kettles before they could be restarted—and it could be done that quickly only if the same exact mixture were being produced.

A three-shift operation can be very efficient if the quality and efficiency of the product is consistent. When very highly skilled workers are required, the efficiency and quality of the work done on the second and third shifts might be unacceptable.

Every factor affecting the decision to have a one-, two-, or three-shift operation will have an impact on the product's profit margin. It is in evaluating these factors and making this and other similar decisions that the DuPont formula is so valuable, as we shall see.

2 and 3. Revenue

Given the assets dedicated to the profit center, how much business can it generate? The issues here include efficiency, how much value added is built into the product, and how much of the process is outsourced. Companies that outsource the total production process, such as warehouse distributors, can expand their revenues significantly with minimal additional investment in fixed assets. Only inventory and accounts receivable will need to be increased.

4 and 5. After-Tax Cash Flow (ATCF)

Given the revenue generated by the business (items 2 and 3), how much profit can be achieved? This is related to the type of business, economies of scale, capacity utilization, and operating efficiencies. It is greatly affected by the degree of vertical integration and value-added processes.

Return on Assets: Its Components

The return on assets ratio is really a combination of two ratios, revenue/assets and ATCF/revenue.

Revenue/assets is called *asset turnover*. It is conceptually the same as inventory turnover except that it encompasses all assets. The second ratio, ATCF/revenue, is known as the *margin*. Multiplying asset turnover times margin yields the return on assets. The value of the DuPont formula far exceeds that of its individual components, however. Many business decisions cause the two ratios, turnover and margin, to move in opposite directions. Therefore, breaking return on assets into these two ratios not only provides a valuable tool for measuring the performance of the SBU, it also gives the SBU a tool that it can use in making decisions.

Here are some examples:

Outsourcing improves turnover but reduces the margin, as profit that was formerly kept in-house now must be paid to the supplying vendor.

Vertical integration improves margins because the company keeps the profit that is achieved at each step of the operation. However, asset turnover declines because additional equipment will be needed to produce the product.

Continuous 24-hour operation reduces the amount of equipment needed; hence turnover improves. Interestingly, margins may also improve because having fewer machine startups may improve efficiency. However, if sales don't keep pace with the continuous output, inventory may build up dangerously, and margins may then deteriorate as a result of price cutting to get the product out the door.

Using the DuPont formula helps in the two main business activities:

Measuring performance
Management decision making

However, it does not make the decision. Valuable as it may be, it is merely a tool. Management must make its judgments on the basis of what the expected result will be if the decision is made.

As the next phase of developing the use of this tool, we will look at three SBUs within a company in order to get a better understanding of the DuPont formula. Their respective results for the past year are given in Exhibit 7-1.

> *Line 1: Revenue.* All three businesses achieved significant revenue gains in the most recent year. The Eisen Company is the largest of the three, with $50 million in annual revenues, while the Norelli Company is the smallest, with revenues amounting to $10 million.
>
> *Line 2: After-tax cash flow.* This is each business's net income plus depreciation expense, which is added back to calculate the cash flows generated.
>
> *Line 3: Total assets.* This identifies the total assets dedicated to each business. Ideally, common property is excluded from this measure and no overhead expenses are allocated to the individual businesses.
>
> *Line 4: Margin.* This is ATCF/revenue. As we have discussed, this measures efficiency and reflects all of the operating decisions made by the SBU management team. Notice that Wilson has the highest (which is not necessarily the best) margin.
>
> *Line 5: Asset turnover.* All three of these businesses are quite asset-intensive. Any asset turnover ratio below 2.0 indi-

Exhibit 7-1. Measurement of Profit Centers Using Return on Assets (000)

	Wilson	*Eisen*	*Norelli*
1. Revenue	$27,000	$50,000	$10,000
2. After-Tax Cash Flow	$1,810	$3,000	$500
3. Total Assets	$20,272	$50,000	$5,000
4. Cash Flow as a % of Revenue	6.7%	6.0%	5.0%
5. Asset Turnover	1.33×	1.00×	2.00×
6. Return on Assets (line 4 × line 5)	8.9%	6.0%	10.0%

cates a considerable investment in assets relative to the amount of revenue earned with those assets.

Line 6: Return on assets. This is line 4 × line 5. It can also be calculated by dividing line 2 by line 3. Wilson has the highest margin (line 4) and an asset turnover of 1.33. Its asset intensiveness is compensated for by the higher margin.

Corporate management now has a tool that it can use to evaluate the performance of these three SBUs. The SBU management teams also have a decision-making tool. The consistent use of this tool provides both clear measurement and an understanding of whether decisions will improve the performance of the company.

Let us be very clear that we are not trying to compare the three SBUs with each other. We do not know what businesses they are in or even if they are in related industries. Eisen Company's performance within its industry may be superior to Norelli Company's performance within its industry. The corporate team, however, may use these measures in deciding how much money to allocate to each company in the future.

There are many adaptations of the ROA formula. They are conceptually the same. Here are some of them:

- Return on capital employed (ROCE)
- Return on invested capital (ROIC)
- Return on assets managed (ROAM)
- Return on net assets (RONA)

In Exhibit 7-1, after-tax cash flow was used. Net income would have been almost as good. Operating income is often used as the measure of achievement. This is helpful if corporate management wants to remove interest expense and taxes from the equation. The premise is that SBUs are not responsible for debt financing or corporate income taxes. Therefore, their measurement should not include these corporate expenses. Gross profit is a very useful measure when individual products or product lines are being analyzed as profit centers. Some companies and analysts use EBITDA as the measure of operating performance. This is a pretax cash flow number that recognizes that financing and taxes are issues to be dealt with at the corporate level, not by the SBU.

Sales Territories

The DuPont formula can also be applied to the management of sales territories within a profit center. It gives each sales team the opportunity to make certain decisions in response to specific competitive pressures. It allows for dissimilarities of strategy if this is appropriate. Company policies that limit the decisions that the SBUs may make can be developed in order to protect the company. Within these limits, each sales team remains totally accountable for its decisions and performance. A financial relationship is created between the sales organization and the manufacturing operation. In this example, there are three sales territories and one manufacturing entity. To keep the example simple, it is a one-product business. Exhibit 7-2 shows the actual results for a recent year.

1. Actual revenue results are reported.
2. Within guidelines set by the company, each territory purchases what it believes it will need. Customer service issues and the size and logistics of the territory have a great impact on that decision

    The sales territories "purchase" the product from the factory for a predetermined price of $1.00 per unit. This is a market-oriented price that provides the factory with a profit.
3. The gross profit is reported. Although each territory paid the same purchase price of $1.00 (line 2), the selling prices are different, and therefore the gross profit percentages are different. The West territory probably sells larger quantities per order, resulting in lower prices and therefore lower margins. Central has higher margins than the other two territories. This may be explained by superior performance, less competition, or a combination of these factors.
4. Territory management expends the funds that it feels are necessary to sell to and service the marketplace. North

Exhibit 7-2. Sales Territories as Profit Centers

		Full Year Results 2001		
	North	Central	West	Factory
1. Revenue	$3,600	$2,400	$1,500	$1.00/unit
2. -COGS ($1.00/unit)	2,592	1,600	1,125	$0.60
3. Gross Profit	$1,008	$ 800	$ 375	$0.40
	(28%)	(33%)	(25%)	(40%)
4. Less: Specific Expenses:				
Sales Compensation	$ 400	$ 250	$ 150	
Travel and Entertainment	75	75	25	
Field Sales Office	50	50	25	
Bad Debts	—	25	—	
Total Expenses	$ 525	$ 400	$ 200	$
5. Profit Center Earnings	$ 483	$ 400	$ 175	$
Invested Capital:				
6. Accounts Receivable	$1,200	$ 800	$ 300	$
7. Finished Goods Inventory	600	800	250	$
8. Total Assets	$1,800	$1,600	$ 550	$
9. Earnings as a % of				
Revenue	13.4%	16.7%	11.7%	
10. Asset Turnover	2.0×	1.5×	2.73×	
11. Return on Assets	26.8%	25.0%	31.9%	

may have more salespeople and/or may pay higher commissions because of competitive issues. Notice that Central has been charged with bad debts. Because the territories may use easier credit terms as part of the marketing mix, they are held accountable if customers do not pay.

5. Profit center earnings are reported. This is:

Revenue − Cost of Goods Sold = Gross Profit − Specific Expenses = Profit Center Earnings

6. Accounts receivable: Each territory is responsible for the credit that it grants to its customers. The corporate accounting department can do all the credit checking and

administration, but the territory makes the final decision about a potential customer's creditworthiness, subject to some debate. Therefore, the territory is held accountable.

7. Inventory: Based upon their sales forecasts, territories order product from the factory. The sales territories are responsible for their forecasts. The inventory that they have on their books is a combination of products that they did not sell and products that they want available for fast delivery. Territories must determine the inventory level that they must maintain in order to keep their ability to deliver competitive. They are each responsible for this strategy.

   This approach does not require sales territories to physically manage the product in the warehouse. It does, however, hold them accountable for the levels and mix of inventory that are maintained on their behalf.

8. Total assets: The working capital (accounts receivable + inventory) managed by the territory.

What is provided here is:

- A clear measure of achievement
- Strategies that are appropriate for each marketplace
- Limitations on extremes to protect the company
- Accountability for those resources used by each SBU that are identified as being competitively desirable

Using the DuPont formula, achievement and accountability can now be measured. Management teams have a decision-making tool that can really help them.

9. Margin: Earnings as a Percentage of Revenue (Line 5/Line 1)
10. Turnover: Revenue/Assets (Line 1/Line 8)
11. Return on Assets: Earnings/Assets (Line 9 × Line 10 or Line 5/Line 8)

   The West territory has the highest return on assets, 31.9 percent. While its margins are lower than those of the other territories, its investment in accounts receivables and inventory is very low. However, while West has a higher ROA, we cannot be sure that it is "better" than the others. There are other issues that need to be considered, including: What is the current market share and potential in each territory? Is North more successful in a very competitive marketplace, while there is less competition in West's marketplace? The DuPont formula is clearly a valuable profit-oriented resource. It can be a key tool for intelligent sales management.

Notice that the factory is also a profit center. It sells to the sales territories at a predetermined, market-oriented price, so that it is given credit or held accountable for positive or negative efficiencies. The factory is responsible for its own assets and is measured as an SBU by margin, turnover, and return on assets. It is accountable for its own inventory so that production runs can be planned to maximize its efficiency.

Chapter 8

Overhead Allocations

CORPORATIONS ARE REQUIRED BY GENERALLY accepted accounting principles to allocate (mathematically distribute or apportion) their overhead expenses to individual profit centers when they prepare information for the Internal Revenue Service (absorption accounting in LIFO/FIFO calculations), the Securities and Exchange Commission, and certain industry-specific regulatory authorities. There are numerous criteria that may be used as the basis for this calculation, including revenue, direct cost, units produced, direct labor dollars or hours, and square footage consumed.

It is presumed, incorrectly, that the methodology that must be used for regulatory compliance is also appropriate for intelligent management decision making. Nothing could be farther from the truth.

Problems That Arise from Allocation

The process of allocating overhead charges to individual businesses can lead to several problems within a company.

It Fosters Politics

The process of allocating overhead charges to individual businesses fosters political infighting. When an executive shines as a result of her contribution to the profitability of the business, this is a positive result. However, when costs are allocated, a manager who knows how to manipulate the allocation methodology can make his department's performance look better by getting charges assigned to other operating units. When one profit center looks good at the expense of another, without the company benefiting at all, that's politics.

It Inhibits New Product Introductions

Accounting methodology assigns a portion of the existing overhead to each new product when analyzing its profitability. This inflates the cost of the new product and causes the estimate of its contribution to profit to be severely understated. The analysis of a new product should include only costs that are incremental for that new product. Existing overhead that is not affected should not be included.

It Understates the Profitability of Business Beyond Budgeted Volume

Overhead allocations are assigned to all products, regardless of volume. When sales surpass budgeted expectations, the accounting department will continue to charge these allocations to the individual products even though the company has already generated enough business to cover the actual corporate overhead. These fictitious charges will continue to be added until the end of the year. This leads to a significant understatement of the actual profits of each business that has had sales above the budgeted number and may cause the company to underreward unit managers who surpass their sales budgets.

It Inhibits Marketplace Aggressiveness

Incremental business is really more profitable than the accounting information reveals. Larger customer orders permit longer production runs and more efficient raw material purchasing. Traditional accounting information does not recognize this.

The ability to give price breaks on larger orders (volume discounting) because of these advantages cannot be recognized because overhead charges are assigned to all products.

It Overstates Savings from Eliminating "Marginal" Products

A company should never eliminate products from its mix except under the following circumstances:

1. The product achieves a negative contribution margin, and there is no opportunity to correct this situation.
2. The product is a quality disaster that will impair marketplace perceptions of the entire business.
3. The company is near capacity and needs the space and machine time for more profitable offerings.

Eliminating a product with a positive cash flow results in the loss of that cash flow. Why is there confusion about this? Because our accounting systems tell us that eliminating a product will save the variable labor costs and the corresponding overhead assigned to the product. Labor costs, as anyone who has ever managed a factory will tell you, are more fixed than variable. They will not be reduced appreciably, if at all, when volume declines. And overhead will not be reduced because the building does not get smaller, nor do the staff departments (including accounting).

What About the IRS and GAAP?

Companies should continue to comply with their accounting responsibilities. Nothing that we are advocating here addresses regulatory issues at all. We are simply arguing that marketing and operating managers should receive the product and performance information that they need in order to make intelligent business decisions and judgments.

Effect on Profit of Different Allocation Methods

To explore these issues, let's look at a company with three profit centers.

Exhibit 8-1 shows the annual results achieved by the Middlesex Products Company. The company is very profitable and serves its customers well. Each of the three profit centers focuses on a distinct marketplace and performs as a semi-independent unit.

Revenue

Each profit center has developed a pricing structure that fits with what is necessary and desirable in its marketplace. Some profit centers sell directly, whereas others sell through distributors or reps. The product mixes will certainly be different. For purposes of convenience, we will assume that each strategic business unit has sold 100,000 units of product.

Direct Costs

This includes all profit center costs and expenses:

1. These costs are *specifically identifiable* to an individual profit center. They include the costs of producing the product, operating and staff expenses, and the costs of any services or functions that the profit center outsources to others.
2. These expenditures are *incremental* to the profit center.

Exhibit 8-1. Middlesex Products Company Income Statement

Full Year 2002

Product/Brand	A	B	C	Total
Units Sold	100,000	100,000	100,000	300,000
Average Price	$15.00	$20.00	$10.00	
Revenue	$1,500,000	$2,000,000	$1,000,000	$4,500,000
Direct Costs	900,000	1,300,000	800,000	3,000,000
Gross Profit	$ 600,000	$ 700,000	$ 200,000	$1,500,000
	(40%)	(35%)	(20%)	(33%)
Corporate Overhead				$1,000,000
Corporate Profit				$ 500,000

They are not shared among the profit centers, and so they would disappear if the responsible profit center were not in business.

3. These costs may be *fixed or variable.* They can be part of the product, or they can be support costs. They could include engineering, product design, and accounting, if these were dedicated to an individual profit center.

4. The profit center management team must have some ability to *control* the costs for which it is responsible. While the management team does not control the purchase price of a natural resource, it can control the quantity purchased, mode of transportation, product source, and whether there is any value added to what is purchased.

Corporate Overhead

This includes all the support efforts that are necessary if the entire organization is to function, such as accounting, legal, corporate staff, and management information systems. It also includes all spending that supports all of the profit centers combined and is really not divisible among them. For example, if all the profit centers were housed in a single building, this building would be considered part of the corporate overhead.

Profit

Gross profit percentages are gross profit dollars divided by revenue.

Corporate profit is the cumulative gross profit of all of the businesses less corporate overhead.

An examination of how overhead allocations affect the perceptions of performance will be very valuable at this point.

Overhead Allocation

If the corporate overhead is allocated on the basis of revenue, the result will be:

	A	B	C	Total
Gross Profit	$600,000	$700,000	$200,000	$1,500,000
Overhead	333,000	444,000	223,000	1,000,000
"Profit"	$267,000	$256,000	($ 23,000)	$ 500,000

Because Profit Center A provided one-third of corporate revenue, it is charged for the same proportion of the corporate overhead. Remember that these corporate charges are not based upon the services that each profit center receives. The amounts allocated support the entire organization collectively.

Notice that on this basis, Profit Center C is losing money. This profit center contributed $200,000 to pay for corporate overhead and achieve corporate profit. It now must revise its strategy to eliminate losses that it neither caused nor can control. A more damaging result is the feeling on the part of company management that this unit will never be "profitable" and therefore must be eliminated.

If the allocation is based on units sold, Profit Center C will look even worse:

	A	B	C	Total
Gross Profit	$600,000	$700,000	$ 200,000	$1,500,000
Overhead	333,000	333,000	334,000	1,000,000
"Profit"	$267,000	$367,000	($134,000)	$ 500,000

"Turning around" Profit Center C is clearly impossible. While remedies for its problems will be proposed, its days are clearly numbered.

If corporate allocations are based upon direct labor (which is part of direct costs), all three of the profit centers will be profitable, as follows:

	A	B	C	Total
Gross Profit	$600,000	$700,000	$200,000	$1,500,000
Overhead	450,000	400,000	150,000	$1,000,000
"Profit"	$150,000	$300,000	$ 50,000	$ 500,000

With this method of allocation, all three profit centers have achieved a "profit."

Which method is correct? Is Profit Center C profitable or not? The answer depends upon which method of allocation happened to be selected by the accounting department. All are acceptable in terms of GAAP requirements. The accounting department will study the company's operations and attempt to select the method or formula that it perceives as being most accurate. However, the results will be the same: Decisions will be based upon the statistical method selected. Will these decisions improve the business, as many expect they will? Let's look at some of those decisions and focus on what solutions would be in the best interests of the Middlesex Products Company.

1. *Are all profit centers contributing to the profitability of the business?*

Absolutely yes. Each of the three has a positive contribution margin. Each is more than covering all of the costs and expenses associated with its individual business.

2. *How should Middlesex management respond to excessive corporate overhead?*

Not by passing it on to the profit centers and asking them to figure out a way of paying for it. The best strategy for eliminating excessive overhead is to hold those departments accountable for their own performance and reduce their budgets and/or expect them to increase their achievement. Allocating excessive spending to operating units does not solve the problem. Instead, it asks the profit center teams to solve problems that they did not create and cannot control. Increasing prices and compromising on product quality to compensate for others' inefficiencies are remedies that are no longer available.

3. *In which businesses should Middlesex management expect improved profitability?*

Why not all of them? We do not know, however, if each of the profit centers can improve its profitability to the same degree. Perhaps 20 percent profit growth would be very easy for Profit

Center B but absolutely impossible for Profit Center C. A 20 percent gross profit in Profit Center C's market might be relatively better performance than 40 percent in Profit Center A's market. We would have to benchmark each profit center against its respective competitors to determine what are feasible expectations. Achievement must be evaluated against potential.

4. *In theory, what would be the most favorable product mix?*

If Profit Center A achieves a gross profit of $6.00 per unit ($600,000/100,000 units) and Profit Center C achieves $2.00 per unit, expanding Profit Center A's business at the expense of Profit Center C would improve gross profit by $4.00 per unit (the gross profit differential). Keeping these numbers real simple, the ranking of these profit centers by gross profit dollars is:

> Profit Center B: $7.00 per unit
> Profit Center A: $6.00 per unit
> Profit Center C: $2.00 per unit

However, if you rank the profit centers by gross profit percentage, the ranking changes:

> Profit Center A: 40 percent
> Profit Center B: 35 percent
> Profit Center C: 20 percent

If you check your company's financial statements, you will notice that in most cases, accountants rank product profitability by percentages, although it is their dollar impact that is most critical.

5. *Profit Center C has a gross profit percentage that is below the average for the entire Middlesex Products organization. Should that be a cause for divestment?*

Middlesex Products Company should never eliminate a business with a positive gross profit unless:
   a. The lower quality of its products is damaging the other businesses.

b. Productive capacity is limited and can be used for more profitable businesses.

c. Supporting it requires too much, less profitable investment.

6. *If these three businesses are all profitable, why make choices at all?*

We do not have to make choices among these businesses if:

a. There is adequate capacity to allow all of them to grow.

b. The company can afford to provide sufficient financing to permit all of them to prosper.

c. The ROI for this funding exceeds the company's discounted cash flow hurdle rate (see Chapter 10).

If the answer is no for any of these three parameters, then product mix choices should be made soon. These become strategic issues with long-term answers. Perhaps one of the profit centers should be sold to finance the others. The profit center with the most promising future should be financed by the cash flow generated by the more mature businesses.

7. *How do we evaluate the profitability of a proposed new business?*

Middlesex Products Company is considering the addition of Product D. The annual forecast for this new business is as follows:

Annual Sales	100,000 units
Price	$4.00 per unit
Direct Cost	$3.00 per unit
Incremental Gross Profit	$1.00 per unit

Capacity is more than sufficient to allow this product and the other three to grow for the foreseeable future. Product D is a very good product that has tested well. There might be some cross-selling and other synergistic benefits with the other businesses, but these have not been included.

a. If Middlesex measures product profitability by gross profit percentage, the proposal for Product D will be rejected.

	Company Average	Product D
Price	$15.00	$4.00
Direct Cost	10.00	3.00
Gross Profit	$5.00	$1.00
Gross Profit %	33%	25%

The gross profit percentage for Product D is below that for the company as a whole. Therefore, Product D will bring down the average.

Prioritizing products by their gross profit percentage may be helpful if the company is near full productive capacity and outsourcing opportunities are not available. Otherwise, Product D will bring down the average and not be acceptable.

b. If the company allocates nonincremental overhead and does so on the basis of units, the proposal to add Product D will be rejected.

Product D Forecast:

Revenue	$400,000
Direct Cost	300,000
Gross Profit	$100,000

The company overhead of $1,000,000 will now be reallocated as follows:

Corporate Overhead	$1,000,000
Units Sold (including D)	400,000
Overhead per Unit	$2.50
Charge to Product D	$250,000
Projected "Loss" on Product D	$150,000 ($100,000 − $250,000)

c. If Middlesex Products Company is most concerned about the cash flow that will be generated by its decisions, the proposal to introduce Product D will be approved.

	Company Without Product D	Product D	Company With Product D
Units	300,000	100,000	400,000
Revenue	$4,500,000	$400,000	$4,900,000
Direct Cost	3,000,000	300,000	3,300,000
Gross Profit	$1,500,000	$100,000	$1,600,000
Corporate Overhead	$1,000,000	—	$1,000,000
Corporate Profit	$ 500,000	$100,000	$ 600,000

Implementing Product D will increase corporate profit from $500,000 to $600,000. Notice that a 10 percent increase in revenue results in a 20 percent increase in bottom-line profitability. This is true even though Product D has a gross margin percentage below the corporate average.

When Middlesex Products Company is reporting its results to others, adhering to generally accepted accounting principles is both required and desirable. It promotes uniformity and integrity of the numbers. This is especially helpful to bankers, security analysts, and others who rely on the company reports they receive. However, the decisions that will improve the performance and financial health of the company are those that improve its cash flow. The methodologies that are best for achieving this objective are different from but not necessarily inconsistent with GAAP. These issues should be explored in your company.

Part 3

DECISION MAKING FOR IMPROVED PROFITABILITY

Chapter 9

Analysis of Business Profitability

THE DISCUSSION IN THIS CHAPTER will focus on the factors that determine the profitability of individual products and help us to improve the decisions that we make concerning these products. We will measure and evaluate the factors that determine the profitability of a product, including:

- Product price
- Unit volume sold
- Costs, both fixed and variable
- Profitability

The financial tool used to achieve these goals is called *breakeven analysis.*

We begin our discussion by looking at the operating budget for Raritan Manufacturing Company, which is presented in Exhibit 9-1. Raritan has established revenue, spending, and profit targets. Note that the costs are broken down by major categories and also separated into their fixed and variable components. Identifying which costs are fixed and which are variable is very valuable for effective decision making. To keep the calculations simple, we will assume that Raritan Manufacturing Company is a one-product business. All of the basic principles of this analysis are equally valid for a multiproduct business. Most of these prin-

Exhibit 9-1. Raritan Manufacturing Company Annual Budget

Revenue (10,000 units × $50 per unit)				$500,000

Costs:

	Fixed	Variable Per Unit	Variable Total	
Direct Material	$ —	$ 5	$ 50,000	
Direct Labor	$ —	10	100,000	
Factory Overhead	40,000	15	150,000	
Administration	45,000	2	20,000	
Distribution	50,000	3	30,000	
Total	$135,000	$35	$350,000	485,000
Operating Profit				$ 15,000

To Summarize:

Revenue	($50 × 10,000)	$500,000
− Variable Costs	($35 × 10,000)	− 350,000
= Gross Profit	($15 × 10,000)	$150,000
− Fixed Costs		− 135,000
Operating Income		$ 15,000

ciples are also applicable to a service business; some of the terminology and processes differ, but conceptually the analysis is the same. The analysis a manufacturing company develops is called a *standard cost system.* This is an accounting-oriented mechanism that attempts to identify how much the company will spend during the budget year under different volume assumptions. In the financial services industries, this process is called a *functional cost analysis.*

After the business has been analyzed using the concepts of breakeven analysis, the actual performance is evaluated as it takes place. This is often called *variance analysis.* Variance analysis provides management with the ability to evaluate actual results against what was expected when the budget was prepared. This both provides accountability and contributes to the learning process. It enables management to determine who is and who is not achieving the goals that the company has set. Also, budget assumptions and forecasts can be retroactively evaluated.

Chart of Accounts

Almost every company has a numerically based accounting system that assigns a series of code numbers to every department. This is very helpful for analytical purposes and is also necessary to comply with generally accepted accounting principles (GAAP). This system ensures that all similar expenses are recorded in the same manner. When accounting transactions are added up at the end of the month and year, the company can be confident that all direct labor has been recorded in one account, all travel expenses in another, and so on for trade shows, advertising, and every other expense. There is no other mechanism that will help us determine how much is actually being spent in each category, which is certainly necessary information. Also, one of the GAAP requirements is consistency. The chart of accounts provides that as well. Note that the five categories in Raritan Manufacturing Company's budget are summaries of perhaps one or two hundred cost and expense codes. And they are only examples. Your company will probably use different categories and may even use different terminology.

Once the chart of accounts is established, the accountants will examine each and every individual cost category in order to attempt to determine whether the cost is fixed or variable. They will often reach simplifying conclusions.

Fixed Costs

Fixed costs are costs that will be the same regardless of the volume produced. They are regular and recurring. The amount spent will not change if volume increases or decreases during a given period of time. Costs included in the category are staff expenses, administration, rent, machinery repair, and management salaries. Note that just because a cost is identified as fixed does not mean that it does not change. Rent can change, as can salaries, employee benefits, and even advertising. These are fixed costs because the amount spent is not volume-driven, although it may be volume-motivated. Advertising and trade shows create revenue, presumably. If this is true, then perhaps a forecast of

weak sales should lead to an increase in these marketing investments. Telephone and travel are examples of other expenses that
may increase when business is soft. Customers may be called and
visited more frequently.

Variable Costs

These costs are volume-driven. They will increase or decrease in
response to changes in production and distribution volume.
Some of the costs in this category are direct labor (production
labor), materials (components of the product), and certain administrative and distribution costs.

Development of Fixed-Cost Estimate

It is estimated that during the budget year, Raritan Manufacturing Company will spend a total of $135,000 in costs that are iden-
tified as fixed. This includes:

Factory Overhead	$40,000
Administration	45,000
Distribution	50,000
Total Estimated Fixed Costs	$135,000

Development of Variable-Cost Estimates

Estimates of variable costs are developed with the help of manufacturing and engineering analyses of the production facility and
administrative departments. Each of the per-unit costs is then
multiplied by the expected number of units to determine the estimates of variable costs, by category and in total. This is described as follows:

Material estimates are based upon engineering specifications, some analysis of production efficiencies, and product mix.
Levels of waste and quality rejects are based upon past experi-

ence, subject to hoped-for and engineered improvements. After consultation with manufacturing staff and, preferably, the people who actually build the product, it is estimated that the material cost per unit will be:

$5.00 × budgeted 10,000 units = $50,000 materials budget

Direct labor is a very complex cost to estimate. Total expenditures in this area may be affected by:

- The use of manual labor versus technology in production
- Outsourcing versus internal manufacture/assembly
- Efficiency
- Number of shifts planned
- Employee training and turnover
- Forecast length of production runs
- Whether the product is market-driven (made to order) or production-driven
- Planned overtime and weekend shifts
- Premium pay agreements

Other Expenses

The expenses other than direct materials and direct labor— factory overhead, administration, and distribution—have both fixed and variable components. The basic premise of the accounting department and others is that while a portion of these expenses is fixed, the balance will increase or decrease along with the volume experienced by the company.

There is serious controversy concerning this conclusion, especially during any individual budget year, when the managers responsible would argue that their costs are essentially fixed. The accounting department would not increase or decrease the number of its own people on a week-to-week basis depending on the number of invoices that have to be sent out. Trucks must cover their delivery routes whether they are completely or partially full. Managers should examine the standards used by their company and evaluate whether the behavior assumed by the cost system reflects their perception of how their costs really behave.

Taking these issues into account, Raritan Manufacturing has made the following estimates of the variable-cost portion of these expenses:

Cost Category	Cost per Unit	Forecast Volume (units)	Variable Budget
Factory Overhead	$15.00	10,000	$150,000
Administration	2.00	10,000	20,000
Distribution	3.00	10,000	30,000

In summary, Raritan Manufacturing's budget is as follows:

Variable cost: $35.00 per unit × 10,000 units = $350,000

$135,000	Estimated fixed costs
+ 350,000	Estimate of variable costs at 10,000 units
$485,000	Total costs in budget

The budget is summarized at the bottom of Exhibit 9-1. Notice that per-unit price, variable costs, and profit are identified on the bottom of the page. The per-unit profit is called *contribution margin*.

Breakeven Calculation

Companies should know the volume they need to achieve in order to reach breakeven. This information should be available by product, or at least by class of product. The breakeven point may be of purely academic interest, or it may have strategic importance. It is particularly significant for very new and, at the other end of the life-cycle spectrum, very mature products. Before we get to mathematical formulas, however, some theory will be helpful.

Conceptually, if Raritan sold no product, it would lose $135,000, which is the fixed-cost commitment. Each time it sells a single unit, $50 in cash is generated. However, in order to sell the unit, Raritan must manufacture it at a cost of $35. The difference between the price and the variable cost per unit is called the *contribution margin.* Therefore, the number of units necessary to break even is the number of "contributions" necessary to pay for the fixed cost. The formula is as follows:

$$\frac{\text{Fixed Cost}}{\text{Price} - \text{Variable Cost per Unit}} = \text{Unit Volume}$$

This formula can be adapted to calculate the number of units needed to reach any desired amount of profit by adding the profit figure as follows:

$$\frac{\text{Fixed Cost} + \text{Profit}}{\text{Price} - \text{Variable Cost per Unit}} - \text{Unit Volume}$$

The breakeven point for Raritan Manufacturing, then, is:

$$\frac{\$135,000 + 0}{\$50 - \$35 = \$15} = 9,000 \text{ units}$$

At 9,000 units, the income statement will be:

Revenue	(9,000 × $50)	$450,000
Variable Cost	(9,000 × $35)	− 315,000
= Contribution Margin	(9,000 × $15)	$135,000
− Fixed Cost		− 135,000
= Profit		$ 0

Now that we know the breakeven volume, there are many valuable observations that can be made.

Analysis 1

Every unit sold will result in a gross profit of $15 per unit. At 9,000 units, the company has generated enough gross profit to pay for the fixed costs of $135,000:

$$\$135,000 = 9,000 \times \$15.00$$

Above 9,000 units, since the fixed costs are already paid for, every additional unit sold results in a profit increase of $15. Therefore, if volume were 9,500 units, profit would be $7,500, as follows:

500 units (above breakeven) × $15 = $7,500

The complete income statement would be:

Revenue	(9,500 × $50)	$475,000
Variable Cost	(9,500 × $35)	332,500
Gross Profit	(9,500 × $15)	142,500
Fixed Costs		− 135,000
Operating Income		$ 7,500

Analysis 2: Price Reduction

This formula can assist in answering a number of business questions. For example, if the company could achieve a volume of 11,000 units (rather than the budgeted amount of 10,000 units), but would have to reduce the price from $50 to $47 to do so, would the price cut be worthwhile?

Revenue	($47 × 11,000)	$517,000
Variable Cost	($35 × 11,000)	− 385,000
Gross Profit	($12 × 11,000)	$132,000
Fixed Costs		− 135,000
Operating Profit		($ 3,000)

A reduction in the selling price of this magnitude with the hope of achieving sales of an additional 1,000 units is clearly not the correct decision. Operating income would decline from a profit of $15,000 to a loss of $3,000.

Analysis 3: Business Opportunity

Let us once again assume a budgeted volume of 10,000 units. Raritan has the opportunity to sell an additional 1,000 units (above budget) through a distributor into a market that it does not currently serve. The selling price to the distributor would be $42 per unit. The distributor would then resell the product for $50.

Think through the issues of selling through distributors versus selling direct. Quality of service might be an issue, and productive capacity and competitive strategies certainly are. Costs per unit and fixed costs will remain as budgeted. Would it be profitable for Raritan to sell these 1,000 units at $42? Assume that without this sale, it will achieve budget.

Financial Analysis Solution

FORECAST

	Without	With	Proposed Opportunity
Revenue	$500,000	$542,000	$42,000
Variable Cost	− 350,000	− 385,000	35,000
Gross Profit	$150,000	$157,000	$ 7,000
Fixed Costs	$135,000	$135,000	
Profit	$ 15,000	$ 22,000	$ 7,000

This example brings up a number of important business issues. As businesspeople, we think *incrementally*. We analyze a business opportunity in terms of how much profit will be added, in this case as a result of the sale of an additional 1,000 units. However, a problem may arise if the analysis prepared by the accounting department is not incremental. Traditional standard cost systems would present the budget in the following way:

Variable Cost per Unit: $35.00

Fixed Cost per Unit:

$$\frac{\text{Budgeted Fixed Costs}}{\text{Budgeted Units}} = \frac{\$135,000}{10,000} = 13.50$$

Total Cost per Unit: $48.50

This accounting practice is called *absorption accounting*. The $13.50 of fixed cost per unit is called the *burden*. If the financial analysis of this sale of 1,000 additional units were done using this accounting convention, the conclusion would be to reject the opportunity as being unprofitable. The analysis would show the following:

Accounting Solution

Proposed Selling Price	$42.00
− "Cost per Unit"	48.50
= Profit (Loss)	($6.50)

How can a deal that adds $7,000 to Raritan's bottom line, increasing it from $15,000 to $22,000, have a loss of $6.50 per unit? This is a question that often creates considerable strife and discomfort, and leads to distrust between the accounting department and the rest of the company.

The answer involves something that we described in the introduction to this book. Accounting is the reporting of the past. GAAP accounting requires that a manufacturing company use absorption accounting. Therefore, in calculating the burden rate, the accounting department is complying with required practices. The mistake is the accountants' belief that a GAAP technique is necessarily applicable to business decision making. The analysis of proposed business opportunities is called financial analysis. Financial analysis involves forecasting the future in order to evaluate opportunity.

Analysis 4: Outsourcing Opportunity

The company is considering hiring an outside firm to do its product warehousing, a function that Raritan is finding very expensive. The warehousing company being considered is an expert in that function; it has an excellent reputation and is interested in handling Raritan's product line. Keeping the numbers very simple, the following information is provided.

Current Warehousing Expense. Raritan's budget includes a fixed warehousing expense of $20,000; this is part of the Distribution budget. The company is doing a decent job and has the capacity to handle up to 12,000 units, compared to its budget of 10,000 units.

Proposal from Warehouse Inc. If Raritan outsources this function to Warehouse, it will save the $20,000 fixed cost. However, the proposed fee is $2 per unit.

The original budget cost structure is:

$135,000 (fixed) + $35 per unit

Removing $20,000 from the fixed cost and adding $2 per unit to the variable cost gives a revised cost structure of:

$115,000 (fixed) + $37 per unit

At 10,000 units, the profit with this revised cost structure will be:

Revenue	10,000 × $50	=	$500,000
− Variable Cost	10,000 × 37	=	370,000
= Gross Profit	10,000 × 13	=	$130,000
− Fixed Costs			115,000
= Profit			$ 15,000

At the budgeted volume of 10,000 units, the profit will remain at $15,000 regardless of whether the warehouse cost is fixed or variable. At 12,000 units and 8,000 units, however, the profits will be as follows:

Units:		12,000	8,000
Revenue	($50)	$600,000	$400,000
Variable Cost	($37)	444,000	296,000
Gross Profit	($13)	$156,000	$104,000
Fixed Costs		115,000	115,000
Profit		$ 41,000	($ 11,000)

If the warehouse cost were fixed, the profit at 12,000 units would be $45,000 and the loss at 8,000 units would be $15,000. At this juncture, it is worthwhile to look at the profits if the warehouse cost is fixed at $20,000 compared to those if the cost is variable at $2 per unit.

| | Profits If the Warehouse Cost Is: | |
Volumes	Fixed	Variable
7,000	($30,000)	($24,000)
8,000	(15,000)	(11,000)
8,846	(2,310)	0
9,000	0	2,000
10,000	15,000	15,000
11,000	30,000	28,000
12,000	45,000	41,000

Every element of these forecasts other than the warehouse cost is exactly the same. This includes selling price and all other costs. There are a number of valuable lessons to be learned from these observations in a variety of business circumstances.

General Observations. *Minimize Losses.* At low volumes, the more variable the costs, the less the amount of the loss experienced by the company will be. At 7,000 units, there will be a loss of $30,000 if the warehouse cost is fixed compared with $24,000 if the warehouse cost is variable. Outsourcing is a definite strategy when volumes are weak, such as during a recession, or when the company is relatively new and the breakeven volume has yet to be achieved.

Breakeven. The greater the proportion of the costs that are variable, the lower the volume necessary to break even will be. If the warehouse cost is fixed, Raritan will have to sell 9,000 units in order to break even. If the warehousing function is outsourced, the breakeven volume is reduced to 8,846 units. This becomes even more critical if the budgeted project has to reach breakeven within a fixed time period or be closed, or if the company has debt or cash flow obligations that require a positive cash flow by a specified point in time.

Economies of Scale. The benefits of size will begin to be achieved when Raritan's volume surpasses 10,000 units. Opportunities to bring outsourced functions inside can then be explored. Before any investments are made, however, all outsourcing contracts should be renegotiated to take advantage of the company's enhanced buying power. Being the low-cost producer is always a desired corporate objective. This can be achieved by continuing to outsource but skillfully taking advantage of expanded purchasing power. Below the breakeven point, the cost per unit of outsourcing will almost always be less than the cost per unit if the same function is performed internally. This is because of the additional overhead and support that may be necessary if functions are performed internally.

Financial Strategy for New Businesses

The profitability impact of what we refer to as the fixed-cost/variable-cost mix is directly applicable to the financial strategy that is appropriate for new business startups. Observe how profits and losses behave with changes in volume from below the breakeven point to well above it. Within the context of profitability (read cash flow) behavior, consider the following truisms:

1. The more funds that are dedicated to the core competencies of the new business, the greater the business's chance for success. This strongly suggests outsourcing as many as possible of those functions that are not part of the business's core competencies. Outsourcing reduces overhead and permits the company to pay for only what it needs. The more the company tries to accomplish itself during these early stages, the greater its fixed costs will be, and the greater the negative cash flows that will surely result.
2. During the early stages of development, the more functions that are outsourced, the faster the startup can begin to deliver its product. The early-stage company that attempts to provide for its own needs—to vertically integrate—must order machinery, hire and train workers and staff, install the machinery, work out the problems, and then begin production and delivery. As long as the company can develop relationships with reliable vendors at

reasonable prices, outsourcing in areas that are not part of the company's core competencies is much faster and has fewer potential problems. This permits the critical focus to be on the customer.

3. When functions are outsourced in the early stages, the costs will be highly variable. Having mostly variable rather than fixed costs at these early stages results in minimizing cash outflows at a most critical time. This allows additional cash to be devoted to marketplace opportunities and the company's core competencies.

4. Outsourcing at the early stages usually results in a higher-quality product. Outside vendors have experience and a track record of excellence. The company's only excellence is in its core competencies and, we hope, its marketing and sales of its expertise. All other responsibilities should be left to outside experts.

5. Keeping costs variable at the early stages expedites the achievement of breakeven. Remember that in the profit table for Raritan Manufacturing, a higher emphasis on variable costs results in a lower breakeven point (8,846 units versus 9,000 units).

6. What happens four or five years later, when having a high level of variable costs appears to be counterproductive? In our example, beyond 10,000 units, fixed costs permit the company to achieve economies of scale. This issue should be considered during the planning process once breakeven volume has been permanently achieved. Prior to that time, the best financial strategy for a startup is to focus its cash and management attention on its core competencies. All other functions should be outsourced to those vendors who are best equipped to provide an excellent product and service at reasonable prices.

Variance Analysis

Analyzing the variances or differences between budgeted and actual results provides the company with the ability to:

- Evaluate past assumptions
- Make adjustments when circumstances change
- Provide accountability for performance
- Revise future plans to focus on current realities

Variance analysis is a management process that involves comparing the actual achievements of the business during a period of time with the budget for that same time period. This process should generally be performed monthly, with more extensive quarterly reviews. The annual review should encompass strategic issues and have a longer-term perspective. To illustrate this process, we return to the budget for the Raritan Manufacturing Company and compare it with Raritan's actual performance for the same time period (see Exhibit 9-2).

Raritan Manufacturing Company budgeted revenue of $500,000 and achieved $547,250. Profits achieved were $45,000 versus a budgeted $15,000. Raritan clearly sold more product and made more profit than was expected. Notice that the third column is labeled *difference,* not variance. Variance sometimes takes on a negative connotation, whereas the event may not be negative at all. The column also has no label of better (worse) because that also has a negative association that may or may not be valid.

Exhibit 9-2. Raritan Manufacturing Company
Full Year Actual Versus Budget

	Budget	*Actual*	*Difference*
Volume (units)	10,000	11,000	1,000
Price	$ 50.00	$ 49.75	$ 0.25
Revenue	$500,000	$547,250	$47,250
Costs:			
Direct Material	$ 50,000	$ 52,250	$ 2,250
Direct Labor	100,000	111,000	11,000
Factory Overhead	190,000	195,000	5,000
Administration	65,000	64,000	1,000
Distribution	80,000	80,000	—
Total Costs	$485,000	$502,250	
Profit	$ 15,000	$ 45,000	$30,000

All differences should be analyzed to see what actually happened; then it can be determined whether the event was "good" or "bad."

Price and Volume

The product was sold at a price of $49.75 versus a budgeted price of $50.00. On the surface, this would appear to be an unfavorable event until you add in the fact that 11,000 units were sold compared with the budget of 10,000 units. While a higher price would always be preferable, the additional units might not have been sold if the price had not been lowered. In fact, if the price had been held at $50.00, actual volume might have fallen below the budgeted amount. Price charged and volume sold are not separate, isolated events. We therefore cannot evaluate them independently, out of context. Revenue amounted to $547,250, $47,250 above budget. While this in itself is certainly a positive outcome, the real analysis involves the determination of how this affected the rest of the business and whether the company's strategy (if there was one) improved the company's overall business performance (it did).

Direct Material

Direct material was budgeted at $50,000, or a variable cost of $5.00 per unit. Had the cost per unit remained at the budgeted level, the actual cost would have amounted to $55,000:

Actual Volume × Budgeted Cost per Unit = Expected Cost
11,000 × $5.00 = $55,000

Since the actual cost per unit was $4.75 ($52,250/11,000), Raritan actually reduced its average material cost per unit by $0.25 compared with the budgeted level. Thus the company reduced cost and improved profit in this cost center by $2,250 because of efficiency. The explanations for how this may have been accomplished include the following:

1. Purchasing larger quantities of product from vendors may have reduced acquisition costs.

2. Longer production runs may have reduced the number of machine setups, improving efficiency and reducing product waste.

Direct Labor

Direct labor is also budgeted as a variable cost. The company expected to spend $100,000 but actually spent more, $111,000. Had the cost per unit remained at the budgeted level of $10.00, the company would have spent $110,000. It actually spent $1,000 more than that amount.

Actual Volume × Budgeted Cost per Unit = Expected Cost
11,000 × $10.00 = $110,000

Actual cost per unit was $111,000/11,000, or $10.09. This $0.09 unfavorable difference cost the company $1,000, which is also:

$$ \$111,000 - \$110,000 $$

This negative event is certainly undesirable. The following factors should be considered and evaluated.

1. If higher volumes resulted in longer production runs, this should have reduced the number of machine setups. If this were true, average labor cost per unit should have been lower than budget rather than higher.
2. If the additional volume were gradual and anticipated, production planning should have provided for the increase, and the cost overrun should not have occurred.
3. If the demand for higher volumes were accommodated by reducing finished goods inventory, then labor cost should not have differed from the budget at all.
4. If the increased volume were a sudden surge, especially if one or two customers placed orders with short lead times, overtime or weekend work might have been necessary if the company was to respond in a timely manner.
5. If the additional volume were from new customers, delivery lead times might have been artificially shortened to

make a good impression. If these new customers placed smaller orders in order to test Raritan's quality or its commitment to customer service, labor efficiency would be expected to decline somewhat.

(Since direct material costs were down and direct labor costs were up, another possible explanation is that the cheaper materials were of lower quality, and thus more labor was required to maintain the quality of the final product. Though this is conceptually accurate, the levels of quality are essentially no longer negotiable.)

Intelligent analysis requires that no judgments be made until the cause of the event has been determined. While differences should be explained, the effort should not be limited to "negative" variances, and no value judgments should be made until the facts are known. Much of direct labor is really fixed. Higher volumes are therefore expected to reduce the average cost per unit. The so-called efficiency explanations really come down to better utilization of a relatively fixed cost. This was not Raritan's experience.

Factory Overhead

This expense category has both fixed and variable components. Based on production of 10,000 units, Raritan expected to spend $190,000 on this category. Breaking that amount into its fixed and variable portions, the budgeted amount was:

$$\$40,000 + \$15 \text{ per unit}$$

With actual volume at 11,000 units, it would be reasonable to expect that expenditures in this category would amount to $205,000:

$$\$40,000 + \$15 \,(11,000) = \$40,000 + \$165,000 = \$205,000$$

Actual expenditures were $195,000. This suggests efficiency greater than that reflected in the budget and a positive variance of $10,000. Explanations for the differences in this and other categories must include the perception that a higher percentage of cost than the standards suggest is really fixed. Other explanations include the benefits of economies of scale associated with the higher volumes. Further examination of the details of the components of this category is required. Surface appearances do not suggest any major problem issues.

Administration

Raritan expected to spend $65,000 in this category based upon the budgeted volume of 10,000 units. The actual budget is:

$$\$45,000 + \$2(10,000) = \$65,000$$

If this category truly has a variable component, it would be expected that at 11,000 units, spending would have amounted to $67,000, calculated as follows:

$$\$45,000 + \$2(11,000) = \$45,000 + \$22,000 = \$67,000$$

The actual spending of $64,000 is even below the original budgeted amount. We know that technology is improving the efficiency of support departments, especially accounting. This might be a factor here.

Distribution

There is opportunity for significant efficiencies and economics of scale in this category, which include warehousing and trucking. Loading additional volume onto delivery trucks costs very little more, especially if the product is destined for the same customers. An efficiently organized and managed warehouse should be able to handle significant increases in volume with very little additional spending. This would not be true if the additional volume were not anticipated, but was very sudden and had short lead times. Disruptions can be very expensive, however worthwhile they may be. The company expected to spend $80,000 in these categories. The budget is:

$$\$50,000 + \$3(10,000) = \$80,000$$

At the actual volume, total spending on distribution could have been $83,000:

$$\$50,000 + \$3(11,000) = \$50,000 + \$33,000 = \$83,000$$

Actual expenditures in this category amounted to $80,000. This represents an efficiency variance of $3,000.

Further analysis of Raritan's performance requires that we dig deeper into the details. All categories should be reviewed periodically to identify both positive and negative events; then the negative events should be corrected and the positive reinforced. The quarterly reviews should be more extensive than the monthly review meetings, unless it is determined at a monthly meeting that the actual results are a significant departure from budget assumptions.

Total actual spending amounted to $502,250. Had the actual variable costs per unit been the same as the budgeted costs, this amount would have been $525,000. The conclusion here is that Raritan generally handled the additional business well, functioned efficiently, and enjoyed some economies of scale that were not necessarily reflected in the budget formulas.

Chapter 10

Return on Investment

AN INVESTMENT IS AN EXPOSURE of cash that has the objective of producing cash inflows in the future. The worthiness of an investment is measured by how much cash the investment is expected to generate.

The analysis of return on investment is a financial forecasting tool that assists the business manager in evaluating whether a proposed investment opportunity is worthwhile within the context of the company's business objectives and financial constraints.

What Is Analyzed?

The investments to be analyzed have some of the following characteristics:

- A major amount of money is involved.
- The financial commitment is for more than one year.
- Cash flow benefits are expected to be achieved over many years.
- The strategic direction of the company may be affected.
- The company's prosperity may be significantly affected if the investment is made or not made.

Why Are These Opportunities Analyzed So Extensively?

Investment decisions should be analyzed carefully because such analysis is of assistance in the decision-making process and because the decisions are irreversible, have long-term strategic implications, are uncertain, and involve considerable financial exposure.

Assistance

Forecasting the future performance of a proposed investment requires the analyst to identify all the issues and effects, both positive and negative, associated with the investment. While this does not eliminate risk, it does lead to a more intelligent, better-informed decision-making process. Facts and expectations based upon research and strategic thinking are incorporated into the forecast. The results of the financial analysis do not make the decision. People make decisions based upon the best available information. A capital expenditure requires significant funds and corporate commitment. It is vital that these decisions be well informed.

Irreversible

Operating decisions, such as scheduling overtime or purchasing larger amounts of raw materials, can be changed when the environment or circumstances change or when it becomes obvious that a mistake was made. With these decisions, the need for correction can be readily determined and the actual change can be implemented quickly, with minimal financial penalty. A capital expenditure decision, such as purchasing machinery, can also be changed. In this case, however, the financial penalty can be substantial. Having installed equipment sit idle because customer orders dried up or never materialized can be severely damaging. Changes in customer preferences that are not recognized before assets are purchased and installed can be even more damaging if the company cannot or is unwilling to admit the mistakes and take corrective actions. The discipline of analysis and fore-casting should minimize the occurrence of this type of event.

Long-Term Strategic Implications

Locating an operation in a certain part of the country or of the world, building a factory in a certain configuration, and deciding what kinds of machines are needed and how many are all deci-sions that will affect the way the company conducts its business for many years to come. These decisions may very well contrib-ute to the company's future prosperity, or the lack of it. Compa-nies can face such risks as:

- Critical raw materials becoming depleted
- Rail transportation service being terminated
- Manpower and/or skills shortages occurring

The discipline of the forecasting process forces companies to identify, evaluate, and resolve these risks and vulnerabilities.

Uncertainty

The ability to predict the future is becoming more difficult and complex for businesses. Markets, customers, competitors, and technology have made the need for strategic discipline more crit-ical than ever before.

Financial Exposure

In addition to the uncertainties and risks involved, the sheer amount of funds that must be committed to a major investment requires that all available facts and issues be identified and eval-uated. If additional debt is directly or indirectly involved, the an-alytical process is even more critical. Involving banks or other sources of external financing is often very helpful. Banks are risk-averse businesses. They will not lend money unless they are con-vinced of the merits of the proposed investment. Lenders often protect their clients by identifying risks that the clients had not identified or had underemphasized. In this situation, the forecast becomes a selling document as well as a decision-making tool.

Discounted Cash Flow

The financial tool that is used to evaluate investment opportunities is called *discounted cash flow* (DCF). The different measurements that use this tool in some way are:

- Internal rate of return
- Net present value
- Profitability index
- Payback period

The types of investments that can be evaluated with this tool are:

- Capital expenditures
- Research and development
- Major advertising/promotional efforts
- Outsourcing alternatives
- Major contract negotiations (price, payment terms, duration, specifications)
- Evaluating new products or businesses
- Buying another business
- Strategic alliances
- Valuing real estate

The Principles of Discounted Cash Flow

Let's start out by identifying a number of key conceptual premises of DCF.

0. means period zero, or the starting point of the project.
1. means one year from the start of the project.
2. means two years from the start of the project, and so forth.

A simple example is:

0. ($1,000) cash outflow (parentheses)
1. $1,020 cash inflow . . . no parentheses

Clearly this is not a particularly attractive investment, since if the money were put in a local bank, the return might be 5 percent:

0. ($1,000)
1. $1,050

The bank deposit is also risk-free because it is insured by the FDIC or FSLIC.

Therefore, we have already established two basic principles of DCF:

1. It is measuring profitability.
2. Risk issues are incorporated.

Profit $ = Interest $

Now consider the following financial relationship:

0. ($1,000)
1. $1,200

If this were the purchase of a stock and its sale one year later, the profit would be $200. If this were a bank loan, where you borrowed $1,000 and repaid $1,200 after a year, the interest would obviously be $200.

These are the same concept; the only differences are semantic.

ROI % = Interest %

The return on investment (ROI) on the stock purchase and sale would be 20 percent. The interest rate on the loan would also be 20 percent, as follows:

$$\frac{\text{Profit}}{\text{Investment}} = \frac{\$200}{\$1,000} = 20\% = \frac{\$200}{\$1,000} = \frac{\text{Interest}}{\text{Loan}}$$

The interest rate is the annual fee that the banker charges for the loan. The ROI is the annual "fee" (ROI requirement) that we impose on an investment.

Time Value of Money Concept

Consider the following:

> 0. ($1,000)
> 2. $1,200

While the dollar amount of interest and profit remained at $200, the ROI and interest rate declined to approximately 10 percent. Therefore, ROI and interest rates are annual concepts.

Discounted cash flow is based upon the *time value of money* concept. What this means is that we not only value how much cash flow is generated, but also are very concerned with when it is received—its timing. Sooner is better.

Principal First

The following two investments are not the same:

	A	B
0.	($1,000)	($1,000)
1.	$1,200	$ 200
2.		$ 200

Notice that the ROI in alternative B is negative. In fact, the figures for alternative B show a loss of $600. For an ROI to be achieved at all, a return of the investment itself must come first. In the case of a loan, the banker wants the principal to be repaid before the interest is recognized.

Discounted Cash Flow Measures

The basic premises of discounted cash flow have now been identified.

1. It is measuring profitability.
2. Risk issues are incorporated.
3. Profit $ = Interest $.
4. ROI % = Interest %.
5. It is an annual concept.
6. Principal must be returned first.

While these key points are all interdependent, the critical one is that interest rate and ROI are calculated in the same way. The basis of discounted cash flow technique is to use present value tables to calculate ROI. Focus on the analysis in Exhibit 10-1. Each lettered item in the analysis is addressed individually.

(a) The company is considering an investment of $15,000. It wants to buy a machine that will help it to increase revenue and the resulting cash flow by enabling it to add more features and benefits to its products.
(b) The company estimates that this opportunity will benefit it for four years. This might be determined by the physical life of the machine, the market life of the features and benefits the machine will make possible, or the market life of the product line itself. Alternatively, the company's forecasting horizon may be four years. The time period involved may very well be determined by the company's comfort level.
(c) The company has determined that the minimum required return on investment for this particular opportu-

Exhibit 10-1.

| | Cash Flows | | Present Value | |
			Factors @ 15%	Amount
0.	($15,000) **(a)**		**(c)**	**(e)**
1.	$ 6,000	×	0.86957 **(d)** =	$ 5,217
2.	6,000	×	0.75614 =	4,536
3.	6,000	×	0.65752 =	3,945
4.	**(b)** 6,000	×	0.57174 =	3,430
			2.8550 **(f)**	$17,128 **(e)**

nity is 15 percent. The company may or may not use the same required level of ROI for all projects. Some companies call the required ROI the *hurdle rate* (that must be "jumped over" by the project). The hurdle rate may or may not be the same as the company's cost of capital. There are many different versions of this terminology, so be careful.

ROI and interest rate are the same. Therefore, 15 percent is also the interest rate. The annual fee that the company will "charge" the project for the use of the company's money is the equivalent of the annual fee that the bank charges for a loan. The 15 percent is also the *time value of money* (TVOM) of that annual fee. In terms of discounted cash flow technique, the 15 percent is called the *factor. ROI, interest rate, TVOM,* and *factor* are four synonymous terms.

(d) These decimals are the present value factors. The decimal given for each year is 15 percent less than the decimal given for the previous year. These factors can all be found in Table 10-1.

(e) The annual cash flow forecast is multiplied by the present value factors. The results are the present value amounts. Through this procedure, each year's forecast cash inflow is penalized by 15 percent times the number of years the company will have to wait for that cash inflow. We are in fact "discounting the cash flows"—hence the name of this technique. The four cash inflows add up to $17,128. This is called the *present value of the cash inflows.* It is, in fact, the value of the deal. If this company invested $17,128 and achieved cash inflows of $6,000 per year for four years, the ROI would be exactly 15 percent. In this example, the machine cost less than $17,128. Therefore, the return on investment is greater than 15 percent.

The specific measures of profitability that can be used to evaluate this investment are:

- Net present value
- Profitability index
- Internal rate of return

Table 10-1. Present Value of $1 Due at the End of n Periods.

Period	1%	2%	3%	4%	5%	6%	7%	8%	9%	10%	12%	14%	15%	16%	18%	20%	24%	28%	32%	36%
1	.9901	.9804	.9709	.9615	.9524	.9434	.9346	.9259	.9174	.9091	.8929	.8772	.8696	.8621	.8475	.8333	.8065	.7813	.7576	.7353
2	.9803	.9612	.9426	.9246	.9070	.8900	.8734	.8573	.8417	.8264	.7972	.7695	.7561	.7432	.7182	.6944	.6504	.6104	.5739	.5407
3	.9706	.9423	.9151	.8890	.8638	.8396	.8163	.7938	.7722	.7513	.7118	.6750	.6575	.6407	.6086	.5787	.5245	.4768	.4348	.3975
4	.9610	.9238	.8885	.8548	.8227	.7921	.7629	.7530	.7084	.6830	.6355	.5921	.5718	.5523	.5158	.4823	.4230	.3725	.3294	.2923
5	.9515	.9057	.8626	.8219	.7835	.7473	.7130	.6806	.6499	.6209	.5674	.5194	.4972	.4761	.4371	.4019	.3411	.2910	.2495	.2149
6	.9420	.8880	.8375	.7903	.7462	.7050	.6663	.6302	.5963	.5645	.5066	.4556	.4323	.4104	.3704	.3349	.2751	.2274	.1890	.1580
7	.9327	.8706	.8131	.7599	.7107	.6651	.6227	.5835	.5470	.5132	.4523	.3996	.3759	.3538	.3139	.2791	.2218	.1776	.1432	.1162
8	.9235	.8535	.7894	.7307	.6768	.6274	.5820	.5403	.5019	.4665	.4039	.3506	.3269	.3050	.2660	.2326	.1789	.1388	.1085	.0854
9	.9143	.8368	.7664	.7026	.6446	.5919	.5439	.5002	.4504	.4241	.3606	.3075	.2843	.2630	.2255	.1938	.1443	.1084	.0822	.0628
10	.9053	.8203	.7441	.6756	.6139	.5584	.5083	.4632	.4224	.3855	.3220	.2697	.2472	.2267	.1911	.1615	.1164	.0847	.0623	.0462
11	.8963	.8043	.7224	.6496	.5847	.5268	.4751	.4289	.3875	.3505	.2875	.2366	.2149	.1954	.1619	.1346	.0938	.0662	.0472	.0340
12	.8874	.7885	.7014	.6246	.5568	.4970	.4440	.3971	.3555	.3186	.2567	.2076	.1869	.1685	.1372	.1122	.0757	.0517	.0357	.0250
13	.8787	.7730	.6810	.6006	.5303	.4688	.4150	.3677	.3262	.2897	.2292	.1821	.1625	.1452	.1163	.0935	.0610	.0404	.0271	.0184
14	.8700	.7579	.6611	.5775	.5051	.4423	.3878	.3405	.2952	.2633	.2046	.1597	.1413	.1252	.0985	.0779	.0492	.0316	.0205	.0135
15	.8613	.7430	.6419	.5553	.4810	.4173	.3624	.3152	.2745	.2394	.1827	.1401	.1229	.1079	.0835	.0649	.0397	.0247	.0155	.0099
16	.8528	.7284	.6232	.5339	.4581	.3936	.3387	.2919	.2519	.2176	.1631	.1229	.1069	.0930	.0708	.0541	.0320	.0193	.0118	.0073
17	.8444	.7142	.6050	.5134	.4363	.3714	.3166	.2703	.2311	.1978	.1456	.1078	.0929	.0802	.0600	.0451	.0258	.0150	.0089	.0054
18	.8360	.7002	.5874	.4936	.4155	.3503	.2959	.2502	.2120	.1799	.1300	.0946	.0808	.0691	.0508	.0376	.0208	.0118	.0068	.0039
19	.8277	.6864	.5703	.4746	.3957	.3305	.2765	.2317	.1945	.1635	.1161	.0829	.0703	.0596	.0434	.0313	.0168	.0092	.0051	.0029
20	.8195	.6730	.5537	.4564	.3769	.3118	.2584	.2145	.1784	.1486	.1037	.0728	.0611	.0514	.0365	.0261	.0135	.0072	.0039	.0021

Net Present Value

The *net present value* is a dollar amount. It is calculated as follows:

Present Value of the Cash Inflows	$17,128	
− Present Value of the Cash Outflows	− 15,000	(the investment)
= Net Present Value	$ 2,128	

A net present value (NPV) that is a positive amount means that the actual return on investment exceeds the target rate, in this case 15 percent. An NPV that is negative means that the actual ROI is below the target. If the NPV is equal to zero, the ROI percentage used to do the calculation is the actual ROI.

Profitability Index

The *profitability index* (PI) is the comparison of the actual ROI to the target ROI. Its calculation is:

$$\frac{\text{Present Value of the Cash Inflows}}{\text{Present Value of the Cash Outflows}} = \text{PI}$$

$$\frac{\$17,128}{\$15,000} = 1.14$$

A profitability index greater than 1.0 means that the actual ROI exceeds the target. A profitability index lower than 1.0 means that the actual ROI is below the target. If the PI is exactly 1.0, the ROI percentage used in the calculation is the actual ROI.

In this example, we now know with certainty that the actual return on investment exceeds 15 percent, as the NPV is a positive amount and the PI exceeds 1.0. The NPV and the PI will never give conflicting signals, and there will never be conflicting signals between the NPV and PI and the actual return on investment. Within the realm of normal business forecasting, such conflicting signals are impossible.

    (f) Notice that in Exhibit 10-1, we repeatedly multiplied $6,000 times each individual annual factor. As an alternative, we can add up the four annual factors, giving us 2.855, and multiply this number by the annual cash flow. Except for differences introduced by rounding, doing one summary multiplication will give the same result as the individual calculations. The sum of the annual factors is called an *annuity factor.* Annuity factors can be used only when the annual cash inflows are the same amount; when cash inflows differ, the present value factors for the individual years must be used. The annuity factors for different time periods and interest rates have been calculated; they can be found in Table 10-2.

Internal Rate of Return

Consider the following formula:

$$PVCO = PVCI \text{ Factor } (\%, \text{ yrs})$$

This is the formula for the internal rate of return, which is the actual ROI based upon discounted cash flow technique. This formula is in all computer software dealing with this technique. In words, it reads:

The present value of the cash outflows (investment) will be equal to the present value of the cash inflows when multiplied by the correct factor.

The correct factor means the factor corresponding to the right percentage and the right number of years. We now have a critical formula in which three of the four parameters are known. Returning to the example:

PVCO (investment)	$15,000	$15,000 = $6,000 × F (%, 4 yrs)
Cash Inflows	$ 6,000	
Number of Years	4	

Solving for the factor algebraically, we get $15,000/$6,000, or 2.5. Now we search in Table 10-2 (the annuity table) in the row for 4 years until we find the factor 2.5. Notice that for 4 years, at 20

Table 10-2. Present Value of an Annuity of $1 per Period for *n* Periods.

Period	1%	2%	3%	4%	5%	6%	7%	8%	9%	10%	12%	14%	15%	16%	18%	20%	24%	28%	32%
1	0.9901	0.9804	0.9709	0.9615	0.9524	0.9434	0.9346	0.9259	0.9174	0.9091	0.8929	0.8772	0.8696	0.8621	0.8475	0.8333	0.8065	0.7813	0.7576
2	1.9704	1.9416	1.9135	1.8861	1.8594	1.8334	1.8080	1.7833	1.7591	1.7355	1.6901	1.6467	1.6257	1.6052	1.5656	1.5278	1.4568	1.3916	1.3315
3	2.9410	2.8839	2.8286	2.7751	2.7232	2.6730	2.6243	2.5771	2.5313	2.4869	2.4018	2.3216	2.2832	2.2459	2.1743	2.1065	1.9813	1.8685	1.7663
4	3.9020	3.8077	3.7171	3.6299	3.5460	3.4651	3.3872	3.3121	3.2397	3.1699	3.0373	2.9137	2.8550	2.7982	2.6901	2.5887	2.4043	2.2410	2.0957
5	4.8534	4.7135	4.5797	4.4518	4.3295	4.2124	4.1002	3.9927	3.8897	3.7908	3.6048	3.4331	3.3522	3.2743	3.1272	2.9906	2.7454	2.5320	2.3452
6	5.7955	5.6014	5.4172	5.2421	5.0757	4.9173	4.7665	4.6229	4.4859	4.3553	4.1114	3.8887	3.7845	3.6847	3.4976	3.3255	3.0205	2.7594	2.5342
7	6.7282	6.4720	6.2303	6.0021	5.7864	5.5824	5.3893	5.2064	5.0330	4.8684	4.5638	4.2883	4.1604	4.0386	3.8115	3.6046	3.2423	2.9370	2.6775
8	7.6517	7.3255	7.0197	6.7327	6.4632	6.2098	5.9713	5.7466	5.5348	5.3349	4.9676	4.6389	4.4873	4.3436	4.0776	3.8372	3.4212	3.0758	2.7860
9	8.5660	8.1622	7.7861	7.4353	7.1078	6.8017	6.5152	6.2469	5.9952	5.7590	5.3282	4.9464	4.7716	4.6065	4.3030	4.0310	3.5655	3.1842	2.8681
10	9.4713	8.9826	8.5302	8.1109	7.7217	7.3601	7.0236	6.7101	6.4177	6.1446	5.6502	5.2161	5.0188	4.8332	4.4941	4.1925	3.6819	3.2689	2.9304
11	10.3676	9.7868	9.2526	8.7605	8.3064	7.8869	7.4987	7.1390	6.8052	6.4951	5.9377	5.4527	5.2337	5.0286	4.6560	4.3271	3.7757	3.3351	2.9776
12	11.2551	10.5753	9.9540	9.3851	8.8633	8.3838	7.9427	7.5361	7.1607	6.8137	6.1944	5.6603	5.4206	5.1971	4.7932	4.4392	3.8514	3.3868	3.0133
13	12.1337	11.3484	10.6350	9.9856	9.3936	8.8527	8.3577	7.9038	7.4869	7.1034	6.4235	5.8424	5.5831	5.3423	4.9095	4.5327	3.9124	3.4272	3.0404
14	13.0037	12.1062	11.2961	10.5631	9.8986	9.2950	8.7455	8.2442	7.7862	7.3667	6.6282	6.0021	5.7245	5.4675	5.0081	4.6106	3.9616	3.4587	3.0609
15	13.8651	12.8493	11.9379	11.1184	10.3797	9.7122	9.1079	8.5595	8.0607	7.6061	6.8109	6.1422	5.8474	5.5755	5.0916	4.6755	4.0013	3.4834	3.0764
16	14.7179	13.5777	12.5611	11.6523	10.8378	10.1059	9.4466	8.8514	8.3126	7.8237	6.9740	6.2651	5.9542	5.6685	5.1624	4.7296	4.0333	3.5026	3.0882
17	15.5623	14.2919	13.1661	12.1657	11.2741	10.4773	9.7632	9.1216	8.5436	8.0216	7.1196	6.3729	6.0472	5.7487	5.2223	4.7746	4.0591	3.5177	3.0971
18	16.3983	14.9920	13.7535	12.6593	11.6896	10.8276	10.0591	9.3719	8.7556	8.2014	7.2497	6.4674	6.1280	5.8178	5.2732	4.8122	4.0799	3.5294	3.1039
19	17.2260	15.6785	14.3238	13.1339	12.0853	11.1581	10.3356	9.6036	8.9501	8.3649	7.3658	6.5504	6.1982	5.8775	5.3162	4.8435	4.0967	3.5386	3.1090
20	18.0456	16.3514	14.8775	13.5903	12.4622	11.4699	10.5940	9.8181	9.1285	8.5136	7.4694	6.6231	6.2593	5.9288	5.3527	4.8696	4.1103	3.5458	3.1129

percent the factor is 2.588, and at 24 percent the factor is 2.404. Therefore, the actual return on investment is between 20 percent and 24 percent. In fact, it is approximately 21 percent. Remember that Table 10-2 can be used only if the annual cash inflows are the same amount. If the annual cash inflows are different, the method described here will work, but since the formula will include each cash flow amount multiplied by the present value factor for that amount, more trial and error and number crunching will be required.

Payback Period

The payback period is the amount of time that it takes for the cash inflows from the investment to be exactly equal to the investment. It is a cash flow breakeven. While it is not a measure of profitability, it is a measure of risk. Consideration of the payback period is especially valuable for companies with tight cash flow situations. While the company does not want to shut off investment completely, it needs to focus on those opportunities that will have the greatest positive effect on its cash position. For the opportunity that has been analyzed here, the payback period is calculated as follows:

$$\frac{\text{Investment}}{\text{Annual Cash Inflows}} = \frac{\$15,000}{\$6,000} = 2.5 \text{ years}$$

This measure is sometimes the only tool that companies use to evaluate an opportunity. The problem with it is that, in addition to the fact that it is not a measure of profitability, it treats all cash flows within the payback period equally, without regard to their time value, and it ignores all cash flows after the payback period.

Risk

The psychology of corporate investment risk is very different from that of personal investment risk. When we as individuals are contemplating an investment, such as a stock purchase, our perception of the risk of the investment focuses on the possibility of our losing the funds invested. In a corporate environment, investment risk involves not achieving the profitability improvement that was forecast to justify the investment and gain budget approval for it.

If an ROI of 20 percent is forecast and the ROI actually achieved is 8 percent, there is a corporate credibility problem and an opportunity cost issue. The next time this manager asks for funds, his "failure" will be incorporated into the decision. The manager didn't "make the numbers." Someone higher up will be wondering what investments were not made because of the manager's 20 percent ROI forecast (and 8 percent actual).

Personally, if we invested in a stock hoping for a 20 percent return and achieved 8 percent, we would be somewhat disappointed, but we would still feel relatively satisfied because "we made money." We personally don't have this type of perception and political issues.

Given these factors, there are ways in which a company can incorporate risk into its investment analysis. These are *payback* and *ROI hierarchy*.

As mentioned previously, payback period is a reflection of risk. The longer the time to the cash flow breakeven point, the greater is the uncertainty associated with forecasting the future. A new machine that reduces manufacturing labor and materials could have a payback period of six months. Expanding production based upon a forecast of new products and new customer opportunities involves considerable risk. This type of investment might have a payback period of three years. While the investment might turn out to be wonderfully profitable, there is considerable uncertainty associated with it. Risk can be incorporated into the ROI analysis by creating an ROI target with the payback period as the guiding factor, as follows:

Payback Period	ROI Target
2.0 years or less	15%
2.0–3.0 years	20%
3.0–4.0 years	25%

The ROI target reflects expectations, risk, cash constraints, and opportunity cost. Payback period helps the company to incorporate risk into the analysis.

Another means of incorporating risk is to classify the projects. The company can then create a hierarchy of ROI targets based upon these classifications. An example is:

Classification of Project	ROI Target
Process improvement	15%
New product	19%
New market	21%
Corporate acquisition	25%

Capital Expenditure Defined

As stated at the beginning of the chapter, an investment is an exposure of cash that has the objective of producing cash inflows in the future. Therefore, the amount used for a capital expenditure should include:

- Capital equipment
- Additional inventory to support the project
- Additional accounts receivable to finance increased revenues

It is quite conceivable that capital expenditures that improve the manufacturing process will make a significant contribution to the reduction of inventory. This will be attributable to:

- Improved communication between the company and its suppliers
- Faster delivery times that reduce the need for raw materials inventory
- More efficient production that reduces work-in-process inventory
- Overall efficiencies that reduce the need for safety stock
- Higher quality that permits a reduction in finished goods inventory

The Cash Flow Forecast

All of the incremental revenues and expenses that will be created if the investment is made should be included in the forecast. The key term here is *incremental.* No existing expenses or overhead amounts should be allocated to the project. They already exist and will not be affected.

> Revenue
> − Cost of Goods Sold
> = Gross Profit
> − Incremental Overhead
> = Operating Income
> − Depreciation
> = Net Income Before Tax
> − Income Tax
> = Net Income
> + Depreciation
> = After-Tax Cash Flow

As mentioned above, many investments that will improve manufacturing processes will also have the very positive effect of reducing inventory. Making the process more efficient, especially through the use of technology, can drastically reduce processing time, almost eliminating work-in-process inventory. More predictable, higher-quality production can reduce the requirements for safety stocks of raw materials and finished products.

Characteristics of a Quality Forecast

A forecast is a reflection of the future. The executive who uses the information to make a major decision that involves committing substantial resources and feels comfortable about having done so has been working with a quality forecast. Does the forecast contain all of the available information that is pertinent to the decision being evaluated? Here are some of the characteristics of a forecast that may provide comfort to both the analyst and the decision maker.

Incrementality

All benefits, expenses, and investments that will change as a result of the decision should be included in the financial forecast. That is the concept of incrementality. This includes indirect expenses and the cost of additional support staff. An engineer who must be added to the team to support the product is incremental. So is marketing research necessary to make some marketplace decisions. Any spending is incremental as long as it results from implementing the decision and will not be incurred if the decision is to not implement the project.

The financial forecast should not include allocations of existing corporate overhead. The purpose of the forecast is to identify the financial impact that the project will have on the company.

Forecast Time Frame

With a few exceptions, most forecasts should provide a maximum of five years of cash inflows. Because of changes in technology and global economic turmoil, predicting the future is more difficult than ever. Even though we hope that the new business will last forever, we know that that will not happen. If five years of cash inflows do not justify the investment and permit the company to achieve its ROI targets, the risk factors increase substantially.

Adding years to the forecast can be a form of analytical manipulation, whether intentional or not. More years of cash inflows will increase the ROI. Therefore, using a set number of years for all forecasts assures comparability and objectivity.

Exceptions will include calculating the ROI on such things as pharmaceutical research or the construction of major oil pipelines. These may very well have time horizons of 10 years or even longer.

Accounting Rules

The forecast should respect the accounting rules and practices that will govern the company's reporting over the period for which the forecast is made. This is particularly important as it relates to tax reporting, which will have significant cash flow effects. However, adhering to accounting format requirements is not critical except insofar as cash flow will be affected. After all, the analysis is forecasting the future, not reporting the past.

External Financing

Cash flow forecasts should assume that the investments will be all cash, and the investments should be included in the forecast at the point when the commitments to acquire assets are made. This is true even if the company expects to get financing for the project from a bank or even from the equipment vendors. The project and the underlying risk begin when the commitments are made, which may be long before the cash is disbursed. While the use of external financing sources may be favorable and in fact may be necessary, external financing increases risk. Debt service payments are a fixed cost that increases the company's break-even point.

If external financing is decided upon, the first analysis should reflect the now hypothetical up-front cash investment. This is called the *base case*. The ROI calculated on this basis should exceed the company's ROI hurdle rate. Analyses of financing alternatives can then be compared to this base case. Thus, discounted cash flow analysis becomes a tool for evaluating proposals from banks and other lenders. When the external financing is included in the analysis, the ROI will increase significantly. Financing is in fact postponing cash outflows. The cost of that financing will be included in the revised forecast. The before-tax cost of borrowing should be substantially below the after-tax ROI, thus improving that ROI on the project in its entirety.

Working Capital Investment

As we have said, an investment is an exposure of cash that has the objective of producing cash flow benefits in the future. If a project involves business expansion, additional inventory will be needed in order to produce the additional products, and additional accounts receivable will be needed in order to finance the sales that will be made. Inventory and accounts receivable are investments just like the purchase of fixed assets. They should be an integral part of the project analysis.

Economics and Pricing

Forecasts should reflect current product prices and operating costs. The company should never rely on higher future selling prices to justify current investments.

1. Technology is causing prices to be lower rather than higher as a business expands. Competition on a global scale makes every business vulnerable to increased pricing pressures.
2. If the project implementation is successful, potential competitors will be attracted and will soon be actual competitors. As a result, prices will not be higher. Computers, computer software and operating systems, and pharmaceuticals are prime examples of this. It is very dangerous to invest in a business on the premise that selling prices in the future will be higher.

You should look at the annual economic forecasts published in the major business publications. These are surveys of the country's top fifty economists. The divergence of their expert analyses is eye-opening. The range between the most optimistic and the most pessimistic forecasts of GNP, inflation, and unemployment is extreme. Most of these forecasts will be wrong. Incredibly, these economists are forecasting only one year in the future. If these economists cannot forecast one year accurately, how can we novices impose our economic forecasts on an ROI analysis and expect to be reasonably accurate? The most effective method of dealing with this uncertainty is to assume that the current economic situation continues, perhaps adjusting it for known events extending into the next year.

Establishing the ROI Target

Determining what the company will define as an acceptable return on investment is a very important process. The target ROI may be the result of intense mathematical modeling or, at the other extreme, simply a continuation of what has worked in the past. We will simply use the phrase *hurdle rate* for this target. Using both the term *hurdle rate* and the term *cost of capital* could be seriously misleading. The ROI target used should reflect:

- The cost of raising debt and equity funds, past and future
- The expected risk and the company's ability to tolerate it
- Alternative uses of the funds, such as debt reduction
- The improved profitability necessary if the company is to attain future goals

Exhibit 10-2 outlines a method of establishing a company ROI target (hurdle rate). It incorporates the factors stated previously. The sequence of events is described by the numbers in parentheses.

1. The company currently has a 10 percent return on assets. Notice that it uses a version of the ratio that employs after-tax cash flow rather than the traditional net income. The calculation is:

$$\frac{\text{After-Tax Cash Flow}}{\text{Assets}} = \frac{\$1,000}{\$10,000} = 10\%$$

2. The company is developing a strategic plan that will include a financial forecast covering the same time period. It does this for a number of reasons, including getting answers to the following questions:

   a. What investments can it afford?
   b. Does the plan achieve the targets?
   c. How profitable must those investments be?

   Targeted return on assets for the year 2004 is determined to be 11 percent. This represents a significant improvement from the level for the current year. It should be benchmarked against competitors' returns and should reflect cash requirements for debt service and dividend payments.

Exhibit 10-2. Establishing Return on Investment Target Using Management by Objectives Concept

	2001 Actual	3-Year Internal Improvements			3-Year Capital Budget
		Volume	Efficiency	Total	
Revenue	$10,000	$500	—	$500	
Costs/Expenses	9,400	460	($25)	435	
Net Income	$ 600	$ 40	$25	$ 65	
After-Tax Cash Flow	$ 1,000 (7)			$ 65 (8)	$ 90 (9)
					$ 1,1 (6)
Assets	$10,000 (4)				$500 (3)
					$10,500 (5)
Return on Assets	10% (1)				18% (10)
					11% (2)

3. The capital budget for the three-year period amounts to $500,000. This should incorporate all of the investments necessary to implement the strategic plan.

4. The current asset base amounts to $10 million. This includes cash, accounts receivable, inventory, and the gross book value of the fixed assets. Using the gross rather than the net book value in this analysis is preferable. This avoids the appearance of year-to-year ROA improvement that results from assets being depreciated, making the denominator smaller.

5. Since the company has assets of $10 million and plans to add an additional $500,000, it is forecasting an asset base of $10.5 million in the year 2004.

6. Since the company's target ROA for the year 2004 is 11 percent and it is forecasting an asset base of $10.5 million, it will have to generate $1,155,000 in after-tax cash flow in order to achieve that target. The calculation i

$$ROA: \quad \frac{\$1,155,000}{\$10,500,000} = 11\%$$

7. The company is currently achieving a cash
million annually, and this is certainly exp

tinue. There are two sources of improvements in this performance, internal and external. Internal improvements are those actions that the company can take to improve existing performance that do not require investments or additional capacity. External improvements are the benefits resulting from additional investments.

8. Internal improvements are estimated to add $65,000 annually to after-tax cash flow. This results from the margins on additional sales volume and improved process efficiency.

9. Cash flow in 2004 must amount to $1,155,000. Subtracting from this figure the amount of current cash flow and the amount estimated to be added by internal improvements leads to the conclusion that the annual cash flow generated by capital investments must amount to $90,000, as follows:

Target Cash Flow	$1,155,000
− Amount Already Generated	− 1,000,000
− Internal Improvements	− 65,000
= Amount to Be Generated by Capital Investments	$ 90,000

10. To achieve this amount of cash flow, the return on investment for all projects must be at least 18 percent. The calculation is:

$$\frac{\text{ATCF}}{\text{Capital Budget}} = \frac{\$90,000}{\$500,000} = 18\%$$

This is not a mathematically perfect model, although its flaws do not diminish its value as a decision-making tool. Projects that are implemented in the first year of this three-year plan will probably h their cash flow potential by year 3. However, larger projects re implemented in the third year of the plan may actually from the company's ability to attain the ROA requirement ent, a project that is implemented in the third year will sset base but may not yet be adding to the cash flow. this will have to be resolved. However, using the

18 percent hurdle rate as a guide will result in quite effective decision making.

Analytical Simulations

The internal rate of return formula can help managers answer many business questions and evaluate reward/risk issues. To review:

$$PCVO = PVCI \text{ Factor } (\%, yrs)$$

Example 1: Number of Years.

A company is considering an investment of $10,000 and expects it to produce annual cash inflows of $4,000. If the company's target ROI is 20 percent, for how many years must these cash inflows continue if the company is to decide to make the investment?
Using the formula:

$$\frac{\$10,000}{4,000} = \frac{\$4,000 \times F (20\%, yrs)}{4,000}$$

Remembering your eighth-grade algebra, the factor equals 2.5.

$$Factor (20\%, yrs) = 2.5$$

We now search Table 10-2 under the 20 percent column until we find a factor near 2.5. Notice that at three years the factor is 2.107 and at four years the factor is 2.589. Therefore, this investment opportunity must produce cash flows at this level for almost four years for the company to achieve its 20 percent ROI target.

This investment model might describe a very high tech investment where the life of the technology itself is in question. If the technology will not continue to be up to date for more than three years, then the company may not achieve its investment requirements and should invest its funds elsewhere. This model can also be used to evaluate fashion items or other investments with uncertain futures.

Example 2: P&L Components

A company is considering an investment of $10,000. The company requires an ROI of 24 percent and expects the investment to produce cash flows for four years. What annual cash flows are necessary in order to justify the investment?

$$\$10,000 = \text{Annual Cash Flows} \times \text{Factor (24\%, 4yrs)}$$
$$\$10,000 = \text{Annual Cash Flows} \times 2.404$$
$$\text{Annual Cash Flows} = \$10,000/2.404 = \$4,160$$

Using the cash flow forecasting model, we can now determine whether the product's selling price, volumes, and cost structure will result in annual cash flows of $4,160.

Example 3: Corporate Acquisition

A company is considering the purchase of another company. It is a "friendly" acquisition to the extent that the buyer and seller are sharing information and negotiating. How much should the buyer be willing to pay if it is to achieve its required return on investment of 24 percent? The company's time horizon is ten years.

1. After-tax cash flows forecast by seller	$ 9,000
2. Reduction by buyer because seller is optimistic	− 2,000
3. Synergistic benefits buyer will experience after takeover	+ 3,000
4. Benefits of improved efficiencies that buyer will implement	+ 2,000
5. Forecast cash inflows achieved by buyer after takeover	$12,000

We then apply the ROI formula:

6. Investment = $12,000 × F (24%, 10 yrs)
7. $12,000 × 3.6819 = $44,183

The maximum financial exposure that the company can afford if it is to receive all of the benefits of owning the subject company and still achieve an ROI of 24 percent on the purchase is $44,183. This is not the recommended purchase price, however. The recommended purchase price is calculated as follows:

Maximum financial exposure	$44,183
Investment necessary to achieve synergies	− 7,000
Investment necessary to achieve efficiencies	− 3,000
Maximum purchase price	$34,183

Some additional notes and comments:

Sellers tend to be optimistic because they are trying to sell something. Therefore, the forecasts they provide have to be discounted, as is done on line 2. The biggest reasons for the failure of an acquisition are:

- The buyer paid too much.
- The benefits were not achieved as soon as expected.
- Unknown problems surfaced after the takeover.

Reducing the amount of cash paid up front improves the ROI. Paying for the business over many years both improves the ROI and reduces risk. This improvement can be greatly enhanced through the use of an "earn-out" provision, which involves tying the payments to the achievement of the cash inflows that were forecast. If the seller forecast cash inflows of $9,000 per year, this is in fact what the buyer is paying for. Tying the buyer's payments to the achievement of that cash flow ensures that the buyer will pay for only those cash flows that are actually achieved. It also challenges the credibility of the seller and assures the seller's efforts should the seller remain part of the buyer's team.

Comprehensive Case Study

This case study will provide an overview of the entire process of analyzing an investment opportunity using the discounted cash flow technique. In addition to this overall review, a number of issues will surface that the analyst should consider. These include working capital investment and the impact that product introductions may have on other parts of the business.

Woodbridge Manufacturing Company is considering the introduction of a new product, an especially ergonomically correct computer pad. Sales of one of the company's existing products will be adversely affected. The bad news is that Woodbridge's existing product will lose some sales. The good news is that the sales will be "lost" to Woodbridge itself rather than to a competitor. The best defense is a strong offense. Someone, whether it is Woodbridge or a competitor, is going to modernize the product line.

Exhibit 10-3 gives sales and cost information for both the new product and the product that will lose sales. All the events that are incremental to this decision and only those events are included in the forecast.

Exhibit 10-4 is a forecast income statement assuming that the decision is to go ahead with the new product. In this exhibit, the incremental revenue and gross profit resulting from the introduction of the new product are calculated. The gross profit associated with the old product will be lost and is therefore sub-

Exhibit 10-3. Sales Forecast and Other Information

New Product:

Annual Sales	50,000 units
Product Selling Price	$2.00 per unit
Direct Manufacturing Cost (Without Depreciation)	$0.50 per unit
Marketing Support	$0.25 per unit

Existing Product:

Lost Sales Annually	5,000 units
Selling Price	$1.80 per unit
Direct Manufacturing Cost	$0.60 per unit
Marketing Support	$0.25 per unit

Other Important Information:

Fixed Asset Investment	$100,000
Forecast Life	5 years
Accounts Receivable	30 days sales outstanding
Inventory Turnover	4 times per year
Income Tax Rate	50%
Corporate Hurdle Rate	10%
Depreciation	Straight-line, 5 years

Exhibit 10-4. Forecast Income Statement

	Year				
New Product:	1	2	3	4	5
1. Revenue	$100,000	$100,000	$100,000	$100,000	$100,000
2. Direct Cost	25,000	25,000	25,000	25,000	25,000
3. Marketing	12,500	12,500	12,500	12,500	12,500
4. Gross Profit	$ 62,500	$ 62,500	$ 62,500	$ 62,500	$ 62,500
Existing Product:					
5. Revenue	$ 9,000	$ 9,000	$ 9,000	$ 9,000	$ 9,000
6. Costs	4,250	4,250	4,250	4,250	4,250
7. Gross Profit	$ 4,750	$ 4,750	$ 4,750	$ 4,750	$ 4,750
Incremental:					
8. Gross Profit (4 − 7)	$ 57,750	$ 57,750	$ 57,750	$ 57,750	$ 57,750
9. Depreciation	20,000	20,000	20,000	20,000	20,000
10. Net Income Before Tax	$ 37,750	$ 37,750	$ 37,750	$ 37,750	$ 37,750
11. Income Tax	18,875	18,875	18,875	18,875	18,875
12. Net Income	$ 18,875	$ 18,875	$ 18,875	$ 18,875	$ 18,875
13. +Depreciation	20,000	20,000	20,000	20,000	20,000
14. Cash Flow	$ 38,875	$ 38,875	$ 38,875	$ 38,875	$ 38,875

Line 1. 50,000 units × $2.00 per unit = $100,000
Line 2. 50,000 units × $0.50 per unit = $25,000
Line 3. 50,000 units × $0.25 per unit = $12,500
Line 5. 5,000 units × $1.80 per unit = $9,000
Line 6. 5,000 units × $0.85 per unit = $4,250
Line 9. Depreciation = $100,000/5 years = $20,000 per year
Line 11. Tax rate is 50%
Line 14. Line 12 + Line 13

tracted from the forecast gross profit from the new product. In line 13, depreciation expense is added back to the net income to calculate the forecast after-tax cash flow resulting from the introduction of the new product. Because this is an incremental analysis, it does not include any costs or expenses that are not affected by this decision.

Exhibit 10-5 is a calculation of working capital requirements. This consists of the working capital necessary to support the new product less the working capital that will no longer be required

Exhibit 10-5. Working Capital Investment

Inventory Calculation:

$$\frac{\text{Cost of Goods Sold}}{\text{Inventory Turnover}} = \text{Inventory}$$

Accounts Receivable:

$$\frac{\text{Annual Revenue}}{365} = \text{Average Revenue Per Day}$$

Average Revenue per Day × Days' Sales Outstanding =
Accounts Receivable

New product:

Inventory
$0.50 × 50,000 units = $25,000/4 = $6,250
Accounts Receivable
$$\frac{\$100,000}{365} = \$273.98 \times 30 =$$ $8,219

Working Capital Investment for New Product $14,469

Existing Product:

Inventory
$0.60 × 5,000 units = $3,000/4 = $ 750
Accounts Receivable
$$\frac{\$9,000}{365} = \$24.66 \times 30 =$$ $ 740

Working Capital Investment for Existing Product $ 1,490
Incremental Working Capital Investment $12,979

because of reduced sales of the existing product. Inventory calculations are based upon direct costs, while accounts receivable is based on revenue forecasts.

Exhibit 10-6 is the comprehensive cash flow forecast. It combines the investment of $100,000 plus the incremental working capital required to support the product with the improved cash flows that are forecast to result from introducing the new prod-

Exhibit 10-6. Comprehensive Cash Flow Forecast

	After-Tax	Present Value	Present Value Amounts	
			Investment	Cash Inflows
Investment	Cash Flows	Factors @ 10%	Investment	Cash Inflows
0. $100,000			$100,000	
1. 12,979	$38,875	0.909	11,798	$ 35,337
2.	38,875	0.826		32,111
3.	38,875	0.751		29,195
4.	38,875	0.683		26,552
5. (14,469)	38,875	0.621	(8,985)	24,141
			$102,813	$147,336

Profitability Index:

$$\frac{\$147,336}{\$102,813} = 1.43$$

Net Present Value:

$147,336
− 102,813
$ 44,523

uct, thus combining all the elements of the opportunity into a comprehensive analysis. The capital expenditure is placed as an up-front investment because it must be made before revenue can begin to be achieved. Working capital investment is placed in period 1 on the premise that it will become necessary as operations begin. The analytical life of this opportunity is five years. This is the lesser of the physical life of the equipment to be purchased and the expected marketing life of the product. Notice that the working capital investment is recovered in the fifth year of this forecast. Conceptually, as the company phases out this product, the inventory of the product will be consumed and the accounts receivable will be collected.

Since the new product has a profitability index of 1.43 and a net present value of $44,523, the ROI clearly exceeds the targeted 10 percent.

At 24 percent, the present value of the cash inflows is $106,712 and the present value of the investment is $105,747.

Therefore, the actual return on investment for this opportunity is just above 24 percent.

Additional Issues:

There are many simplifying assumptions that go into a forecast. The first is that the forecast will be achieved. Notice that the working capital investment is placed in year 1. It could be argued that the inventory will be needed before the project starts (in period 0), whereas the accounts receivable will begin in year 1. The statement that the working capital investment will be fully recovered in year 5 is also speculative. Some analysts use year 6 for this recovery, after the project is over. The idea that all of the inventory will be able to be sold at full price in year 5 is also questionable. The solution is to prepare the investment and cash flow forecast with as much objectivity and thought as possible, but to never forget that this is a forecast.

Part 4

ADDITIONAL FINANCIAL INFORMATION

Chapter 11

Financing the Business

BORROWING MONEY IS A VERY positive corporate strategy. It helps the company to increase its growth, finance seasonal slowdowns, and invest in opportunities that will ensure its future. However, while the proper financing strategy will support these objectives, the wrong financing strategy will make what otherwise would be excellent corporate programs vulnerable to failure.

Business and our global economy are very dynamic. They are constantly changing, and the rules are always being redefined. Therefore, financing strategies must also be dynamic. What was appropriate for the company six months ago may be very undesirable now. So, like most other aspects of the business, the company's financing requires constant monitoring and revision.

Those members of the management team who are responsible for marketing, operations, human resources, and technology have no direct responsibility for the company's relations with the financial community, although in a smaller company they may participate in this process when a major project is involved. All senior executives of public companies will be called upon to answer questions posed by stockholders and the financial community.

Every major project of the company will ultimately be affected by the existence, form, and quantity of the financing that the company secures. Budgets are expanded and people are hired because of new financing. Budgets and headcounts are reduced when financing is not obtained or the terms are onerous.

This chapter is included in this book because every business-person has an extreme vested interest in financing and financial strategy.

The main issues affecting financing are its:

- Maturity
- Cost
- Conditions and restrictions
- Payment schedule
- Collateral

There are two classes of financing, debt and equity.

Debt

A company that uses debt to finance its business can engage in either short-term or long-term borrowing. Short-term borrowing involves loans with a maturity of one year or less. It is used to cover current cash needs, such as financing growth, seasonal cash flow needs, and major customer orders. The loans in this category are often called working capital loans, because that is what they finance.

Long-term loans have maturities of longer than one year. Companies borrow long-term to finance major capital expansions, research and development projects with longer time horizons, and real estate.

Short-Term Debt

There are a number of types of both short- and long-term debt, and a number of related elements. We first cover those having to do with short-term debt:

1. Accounts receivable financing
2. Factoring
3. Inventory financing
4. Floor planning
5. Revolving credit

6. Zero-balance accounts
7. Lines of credit
8. Credit cards
9. Compensating balances

Accounts Receivable Financing. This is an excellent form of short-term financing that assists the company in its cash flow management. It involves using part or all of accounts receivable as collateral for short-term loans. The collateral might include only specific invoices if some of the invoices are over 90 days old or if some customers' credit is not of high quality. (If the latter is true, maybe these customers shouldn't be given credit at all.) By refusing to lend against these invoices, the bank is protecting itself from lending against the receivables of low-credit-rated customers. At the same time, it is giving the company some sound advice regarding dealings with these customers.

With accounts receivable financing, the company retains the credit risk if its customers do not pay, and the company is responsible for collecting on its customers' accounts. Repayment schedules for this type of financing are highly negotiable. The company should make certain that undesirable inflexibilities are not built into the repayment terms. There are critical "shades of gray" between financial discipline and bank-imposed restriction. Banks and other lenders will typically create a line of credit equal to between 70 and 90 percent of qualified accounts receivable.

Factoring. In this financing alternative, the company actually sells its qualified accounts receivable to the bank or an independent factoring company at a discount from the face value. The company receives immediate cash for its invoices. The invoices will direct the customers to pay the funds directly to the bank or factoring company (the factor).

This form of financing is expensive compared with alternative forms. In addition, it may lead customers to misjudge the financial position of the company and conclude that it is having financial difficulties. The factor may have the right to take the initiative and call overdue accounts directly.

Factoring can cost between 2 and 5 percent per month. This could significantly cut into margins, especially if the borrower is in a low-margin business. However, if the terms of sale are currently 2/10, n/30, factoring may be a desirable alternative. Selling on terms of 2/10, n/30 means that the customer can take a 2 percent discount off the invoice amount if the invoice is paid within 10 days of the invoice date, and in any event payments are expected within 30 days. With these terms, customers will either take the 2 percent discount or delay payment for up to 30 days. If factoring can be accomplished at 2 percent and the company can get its cash immediately, factoring is an attractive alternative.

Accounts receivable can be sold to a factor with or without recourse. If the sale is without recourse, the buyer of the accounts receivable (the factor) assumes the full credit risk. If the customer does not pay, the factor loses the money. If the sale is with recourse, the company assumes ultimate responsibility for credit losses if the customer does not pay. Selling without recourse is very expensive. Because only very high-quality receivables qualify for this form of financing, there is rarely a credit loss. So selling without recourse rarely pays. Companies can actually buy credit insurance that protects them against credit loss.

Inventory Financing. Usually only finished goods and raw materials inventory qualify as a form of collateral. There is no market for work in process. Lenders will usually provide financing in the amount of one-half of the collateral that qualifies. This is a good form of financing to cover the cost of fulfilling a very large order from a high-quality customer, or perhaps, in a seasonal business, to cover a period of high cash needs that will be followed by a period of high cash inflows.

Using inventory as collateral requires fairly sophisticated inventory control methods, including systems support. This imposes corporate self-discipline, which the company should have anyway.

Floor Planning. Floor planning is a special form of inventory financing that is very common in the retail sale of very high-priced products, such as boats, cars, and appliances. With this form of financing, it is the vendor and its products that must be credit-qualified. The lender buys the products from the manufacturer and places them in the retailer's store and supporting warehouse, in effect lending them to the retailer.

The lender retains title to the products. When the product is sold by the retail dealer, the dealer must first pay the lender in order to get title, which it can then transfer to the purchasing customer. This may be a simultaneous transaction, so that the retailer just receives the difference between the selling price and the loan amount.

Floor planning is often provided by a finance company owned by the manufacturer. The manufacturer and its associated finance company will provide various "bargains" to induce the retailer to overload on inventory. This smooths out the manufacturing process and places a lot of product in the dealer's showroom, which presumably will help sales. Slow-moving product is often provided to the dealer at zero financing cost as a way for the manufacturer to handle excess inventory.

As a business lesson, count the number of cars in a dealer's lot, calculate the estimated value of those cars (maybe the number of cars × $20,000), and multiply that by 1 percent per month (the interest the dealer has to pay on the loan). You can get an idea of how many cars a dealer must sell each month just to cover its floor plan interest expense.

Revolving Credit. This is basically a working capital loan with accounts receivable and inventory as collateral. The maximum amount of the loan is based on a formula tied to high-quality inventory and accounts receivable. For example, the maximum amount might be 75 percent of accounts receivable less than 60 days old and 50 percent of finished goods and raw materials inventory less than 60 days old. This formula forces the company to make regular payments and reduce the outstanding debt when the inventory is used and the receivables are collected.

Because of the pressure to repay and the constant monitoring of working capital, it would be very dangerous for a company to use this form of funding to support long-term projects. Some banks require what is known as a "cleanup" period. This means that for some period of time, perhaps one month per year, the loan balance must be zero.

Zero-Balance Accounts. This type of account may very well be required by another loan agreement. In a "regular" loan, the borrower collects funds from its customers, deposits the funds in the company checking account, and makes some sort of payment to the lender for principal and interest on the loan. With a zero-balance feature, the loan and the checking account are connected. When customer payments are deposited in the checking account, the funds are automatically used to reduce the loan balance and pay the interest that is due. Since the account balance is therefore zero, when the company writes checks, these checks increase the loan balance.

This feature is very similar, conceptually, to the overdraft privileges attached to individuals' checking accounts (although individuals usually decide how much of the funds they deposit should be used to reduce the loan balance, subject to a minimum monthly payment). This feature can be very beneficial to the company because float is reduced to zero. Customer payments automatically reduce the loan balance. The interest rate may also be advantageous because the bank knows that as the company receives payments from its customers, the loan will be repaid. Also, the company borrows only the exact amount it requires.

Lines of Credit. A line of credit is not a loan, it is a very favorable method of securing a loan. The cliché describing this arrangement is "borrow when you don't need it so that you will have it when you do."

Suppose that a company is considering expansion plans or a major expenditure, to take place sometime within the next six months. The company's balance sheet is strong, and its need for the loan is uncertain, or at least not immediate. The company can go to the bank and arrange for a line of credit. This is an advance reservation that makes funds available, to be used only if and when they are needed.

The advantages of a line of credit are:

- The loan is arranged at the timing of the borrower.
- The funds are available; they can be used or not, at the choice of the borrower.
- The company is in a position to make major purchase

commitments knowing that this and maybe other financing options are available.

- It provides considerable purchase price bargaining power.
- Interest payments do not begin until the funds are actually needed.

The company will pay a reservation fee, probably in the range of 1 percent of the total line. Payment terms, interest, and other fees and collateral requirements will be the same as those on any other loan and are always negotiable. This is conceptually the same as a homeowner's equity line of credit.

Credit Cards. More and more customer orders are being placed by phone or by computer over the Internet. Allowing the customer to pay by credit card accomplishes a number of things:

- It eliminates accounts receivable, thus eliminating the wait for the money and the associated paperwork.
- The customer's creditworthiness need not be evaluated.
- There will be no overdue receivables.
- The customers can take as much time as they want to pay.

For smaller orders, waiting for customer payments and making the often inevitable collection phone calls eliminates the profit. Although the company must pay the credit card fee, which is approximately 2 percent, accepting credit cards will make small orders profitable.

Compensating Balances. Requiring compensating balances is a bank strategy that increases the effective cost of borrowing money without increasing the stated interest rate. A compensating balance means that the borrower is required to keep a certain minimum balance in the checking account at all times.

If a company borrows $1,000,000 for one year at 10 percent, the interest rate is obviously 10 percent. If, however, a 10 percent compensating balance is required, the borrower has the effective use of only $900,000. This results in an effective rate of 11 percent. If the borrower really needs $1.0 million, it must borrow approximately $1.1 million.

Along with loan origination fees, collateral audit fees, search fees, and other such charges, compensating balances are a cost of borrowing and can be negotiated.

Long-Term Debt

The following types of long-term debt are covered here:

1. Term loans
2. Bonds
3. Debentures
4. Mortgage bonds
5. Convertible bonds
6. Senior debt
7. Subordinated debt
8. Junk bonds

Term Loans. This is the form of long-term debt most frequently used by businesses. It is a loan from a bank to a company that is used to finance expansion efforts. It has a fixed maturity date, frequently five to seven years from the date of the loan. The company will repay the loan in monthly installments of principal and interest. Spreading the payments of the principal over the life of the loan is called *loan amortization.* The monthly payments of principal and interest are called *debt service.* The amortization of the principal can take place over a period that is longer than the loan period. With this arrangement, the remaining principal is due at the end of the loan period. That ending balance is called a *balloon payment.*

Bonds. A bond has many characteristics similar to those of a term loan. The differences are:

1. A bond is a negotiable instrument that can be bought and sold like common stock.
2. A bond is usually sold to the public through a public offering registered with the Securities and Exchange Commission.

Bonds are usually sold in units of $1,000. A bond that is selling at its face value is said to be selling at *par*. The interest rate is called the *coupon*. After these securities are issued, their prices fluctuate in accordance with economic conditions. The prices of many of these securities are quoted daily in all major financial publications. Bonds are usually interest payments only with principal repaid at maturity.

Debentures. A debenture is a bond with only "the full faith and credit" of the company as collateral. Other than the credit rating and creditworthiness of the debtor, there is no specific collateral. The owners of these bonds, therefore, are classified as unsecured creditors.

Mortgage Bonds. A mortgage bond differs from a debenture only in that there is specific collateral to back up the security. Owners of these bonds are known as secured lenders. Because of this collateral, the interest rate should be lower than that on a debenture.

Convertible Bonds. This is a type of debenture with a very interesting feature. If a company does not have a high credit rating and therefore does not qualify for a reasonable interest rate, it would be prohibitively expensive for that company to sell bonds. Remember that investors and lenders have very different risk/ reward relationships. An investor may take a very high risk in the hope of experiencing a very high reward. A lender can never make more that the interest rate, and thus a lender that takes a very high risk may lose everything without having the prospect of a high reward. The convertible bond changes the risk/reward relationship for the lender.

The bond is sold at a relatively low interest rate, perhaps 7 percent rather than the 12 percent that the company would otherwise have to pay. The owner of the bond has the right to convert the bond into shares of common stock at a later date. The company enjoys an affordable interest rate and can now expand its business. The owners of the convertible bonds get some interest and share in the rewards of success if the company does well and the price of the stock increases to above a predetermined threshold price called the *strike price.* Prices of convertible bonds are listed in the bond price tables in major financial publications with the extra symbol CV.

Senior Debt. This is a debenture issue that gives its holders priority over the holders of all other debenture issues in receiving interest payments and access to the company's assets in case of a bankruptcy.

Subordinated Debt. Holders of this type of debt have priority below that of the holders of senior debt. Because of this secondary position and the resulting higher risk position, holders of this debt will receive a higher interest rate than the holders of senior debt.

Junk Bonds. The creditworthiness of most companies and their securities is rated by various agencies such as Standard & Poor's and Moody's. Generally bonds with the three or four highest ratings are classified as investment grade. Bonds in this category are recommended for pension funds and very conservative investors.

Bonds that do not qualify for these high ratings have a much smaller pool of available buyers. As a result, they must pay considerably higher interest rates, and so they are classified as "high yield." As a company's creditworthiness declines, the yield on its bonds increases at an increasing rate because of the incrementally greater risk. When bonds reach a very-high-yield, lower-quality status, they are known as "junk" bonds.

Equity

Selling common and preferred shares is essentially a permanent form of financing. It is also a form of financing that requires no repayment. In addition to raising funds, equity may also be issued for the purpose of expanding ownership of the stock, reducing concentration of voting power, and making the stock more liquid for stock market purposes.

There are three particularly important categories under the

general heading of stockholders' equity that deserve attention here:

1. Venture capital
2. Preferred stock
3. Common stock

Venture Capital

Investors who supply venture capital are usually financing not much more than an idea, perhaps supported by a business plan. To obtain this type of financing, the founders of a company must be people who have some sort of track record or credentials indicating that they can effectively span the gap between idea and marketable product. Venture capital financing is most frequently available to high-tech ideas.

Venture capital financiers are a very valuable source of early-stage investment funds. The companies they finance are not candidates for any sort of bank borrowing unless the principals or their backers are high-net-worth individuals who are willing to personally guarantee the loans.

People seeking venture capital financing will have a number of fundamental issues to deal with. Venture capital investors will want a large piece of the equity so that if the company is successful, its success will pay for their probable other failures. They will be intimately involved in how their money will be spent. On the other hand, the company founders may very well not have any alternative, and also may not have the managerial and marketing skills to create a viable business. Therefore, unless the company founders have an "angel" investor, venture capital is a very valuable option.

An "angel" investor is usually a high-net-worth individual who finances many start-ups that may not appear attractive to more traditional investment firms. Such an investor often mentors the start-up's management team and provides necessary management and marketing skills.

Preferred Stock

Preferred stock is a hybrid class of equity that is usually associated with mature businesses with considerable, predictable cash flow. The company may have very high investments in fixed assets and may have limited ability to raise money through debt issues. Preferred shareholders receive an indicated, not guaranteed dividend. In periods when cash is tight, holders of preferred stock receive their full dividend before common shareholders can receive any dividend. Preferred stockholders generally are not entitled to vote, unlike common shareholders, but they may have an option to convert their stock into common stock. While interest payments on debt are tax-deductible for the issuer, preferred dividends are not. Thus, for the company this is a fairly expensive form of financing.

Common Stock

A company that is going public for the first time will do an initial public offering, or IPO. By going public, the company can both raise a considerable amount of cash and create a market for the stock. This means that the stock held by the existing owners (the company's founders and venture capitalists) will become a liquid asset, enabling them to eventually sell some of it. Going public is very expensive. SEC filings and legal expenses can cost many hundreds of thousands of dollars. In addition, the equity of existing owners will be diluted, possibly to the point where they will lose effective control.

Many public companies issue additional shares to investors over the years to raise funds, improve the liquidity of the stock, and make shares available to employees.

Some Guidance on Borrowing Money

When a company borrows money, whether it is to finance an expansion, to cover working capital needs, or to acquire another business, preparation is required. It is important to understand that payments of principal and interest will often be required each month.

1. Interest payments are a tax-deductible expense and will appear on the income statement. Repayments of princi-

pal are not an expense, will not appear on the income statement, and are not tax-deductible.

2. Only the principal portion of the unpaid balance will appear on the balance sheet; it will appear as a current liability if it is due within one year or as a long-term debt if it is due in more than one year, or it may be split between the two categories. Interest is never a liability on the balance sheet unless a payment is overdue. This will be referred to as an accrued liability.

3. As previously mentioned, the key issues to be negotiated when arranging a loan are:

The amount: When the company is planning the project, a cash flow forecast is necessary, both for analytical purposes and also to present to the bank. Don't ask for less money than you really need. This may impair rather than improve your negotiating ability. Some people believe, incorrectly, that asking for a smaller amount will enhance their chances of having the loan approved. However, being inadequately funded will hurt the project and may require you to cut back at a time when you are trying to build the business. This is very counterproductive.

The interest rate: Evaluate the issue of a fixed rate versus a variable rate. A variable rate may be tied to the London interbank offer (LIBOR) rate or the prime rate. For example, it may be quoted as "prime + 2," which means two percentage points above the prime rate. If it is tied to a prime rate, make sure that you know whose prime rate will be used. Will it be your bank's prime rate or the rate quoted by the large money center banks, such as Citi, Chase, or Bank of America? Understand that when interest rates are moving higher, they generally move quickly. This is in the bank's best interest. When interest rates are declining, they are often "sticky," meaning slow to move.

The years of payments: The questions involved here are, "What is the maturity date of the loan?" and "Over how many years will the loan be amortized?" The first of these questions indicates how many years of principal and interest payments you will have to make. Make sure that the project being financed will achieve its potential before the maturity date of the loan. Also, if the project is projected to achieve a positive cash flow in three years, where will the company get the cash it needs to make payments in the first and second years? Payments must be scheduled (read minimized) in such a way that they are very low in the early years and then increase in the latter years. This permits the loan to be repaid with the cash flows generated by the project itself. If the maturity and the number of years of amortization are not the same, a balloon payment will be required, as mentioned previously.

Fees, compensating balances, and restrictions: Incorporate all fees into the loan. That saves cash for the project and postpones the payments over the life of the loan. Remember that a compensating balance reduces the amount that is actually available for the project.

Collateral: Keep it to a minimum. Try not to pledge all of your assets. Doing so restricts your future flexibility and creates greater vulnerability should cash flows not grow as fast as expected. Banks usually have loan/collateral formulas. Find out what these formulas are early in the discussions.

4. When negotiating, use your banker as an adviser. Her advice is free, and she is often very knowledgeable. Bankers' conservatism serves as a protective mechanism. Your company has needs and will make substantial profits after your project succeeds. The bank has needs, as well. But its upside profitability is limited to the interest rate it can achieve on the loan.

5. Learn how to use the amortization schedule. An example follows:

Loan Amount	$100,000
Time to Pay	5 years
Interest Rate	8.5%

The monthly payment will be $2,051.65. Total payments over the 60 months will be $123,099, broken down as follows:

Principal	$100,000
Interest	23,099
Total	$123,099

The payments during the first two years will be mostly interest. In fact, after the first year, the amount of principal still owed will be more than $83,000.

The number of years of amortization can be more critical to success than the actual interest rate. If the same $100,000 loan has an interest rate of 9.5 percent (100 basis points or 1 percentage point higher) but is for a seven- rather than a five-year term, the monthly payment will be reduced to $1,634.40. To improve cash flows during the early years, a higher interest rate but longer term will be beneficial.

Consider a twenty-year amortization with a seven-year balloon. This means that the monthly payments of principal and interest are calculated as if this were a twenty-year loan. If this loan had a 10 percent interest rate, the monthly payment would be reduced to $965.02. What this means, however, is that after seven years, the principal amount will still be $84,072.45, and this balloon payment is due at that time. This could be dangerous if the company has the cash to repay the loan in the early years but diverts the funds to other uses rather than preparing to repay. When the balloon comes due, the company's negotiating power is limited or nonexistent. The best strategy might be to arrange the twenty-year amortization and then begin to prepay after a year or two. The company can also prearrange a schedule of two years of reduced payments and then extra payments for years three through seven, after which the loan will be fully paid off.

Chapter 12

Business Planning and the Budget

THE PLANNING PROCESS IS A cohesive management effort that organizes management knowledge, mobilizes the company's resources, and focuses those resources on achieving the company's goals. The first phase of this annual effort is somewhat strategic in nature. It might be best done off site because it requires managers to think about the business and to brainstorm ideas. A database of past information is helpful because there is much to be learned, both positive and negative, from what has happened in the past. Considerable research is required in the areas of:

- Markets
- Technology
- The economic environment
- Competition
- Human resource issues
- Organizational development

S.W.O.T. Analysis

S.W.O.T. stands for *s*trengths, *w*eaknesses, *o*pportunities, and *t*hreats. It is a form of management self-examination to ensure that all of the issues facing the company have been brought to the surface. The results of this self-examination should be action plans that identify:

1. *Strengths:* The best opportunities available to the company. Is the company dedicating adequate resources to these opportunities? Are marketing and operational efforts synchronized? The company must make certain that its strengths are translated into competitive advantage and improved profitability.
2. *Weaknesses:* Issues that make the company vulnerable to loss of market share and reduced profitability.
3. *Opportunities:* Actions that the company can take to improve its performance and achieve its goals.
4. *Threats:* Those internal and external vulnerabilities that can damage the company's future.

The SWOT analysis should cover a variety of areas, including:

- Management
- Products
- Financial strength
- Market position
- Technology
- Operations
- Distribution
- Economic environment

In summary, this effort is a corporate self-examination of where you are, where you want to go, and how will you get there. On the basis of this analysis, action plans indicating what actions should be taken now in order to attain the desired future should be developed. The planning process does not eliminate risk. It attempts to ensure that the right risks are taken for the right reasons to attain the desired goals. Resource allocation is a key component of this effort. Will the most important projects be properly funded? Can crises be anticipated and unforeseen events dealt with?

Planning

There are a number of reasons why planning is necessary:

- The future is not an extension of the past.
- The rate of change in the marketplace will continue to accelerate.
- Technological progress is taking place at an extraordinary rate.
- Regulatory issues require constant attention.
- Population changes, demographics, and geographic shifts require constant adjustment of marketing strategies.
- Global competition is common in almost every industry.
- Business success/failure experience is changing.
- Organizations and the workforce are becoming more complex.

Types of Planning

Here are the types of planning that companies engage in and some key issues involving each:

Strategic: What businesses is the company in, and what businesses should it be in?

Marketing: Why do customers buy the company's products, and why should they? This should also include discussions of pricing, quality, and service strategies.

Sales effort: Should the company sell through a dedicated organization, through distributors, or via the Internet? How can marketplace awareness of the company's products be improved?

Operations: What is the supply chain strategy? How can technology improve customer service and reduce inventory at the same time? What functions can be more efficiently outsourced? How will demographic changes affect the workforce in the future?

Financial: How much free cash flow does the company expect to generate? What are the internal (capital expenditures) and external (debt service) demands made upon these funds?

Requirements for Effective Planning

There are a number of elements that are required if planning is to be effective.

1. Management must provide:
   - Conspicuous support
   - Active participation
2. Goals must be quantifiable. In addition, if they are to be useful, goals must be:
   - Time-related
   - Measurable
   - Attainable
   - Simple to calculate
   - Realistic
3. This is a profit center effort with staff support.
4. Performance expectations should be reflected in the budget.
5. The effort should be relatively flexible and simple. It should not constrain creativity, judgment, and risk taking.

Planning and Management

For planning to be effective, profit center managers need to have:

- A clear understanding of their job responsibilities
- Good leadership through constant, clear communication of plans, goals, and direction
- The opportunity to participate in planning and decision making
- Recognition of their achievements
- A performance appraisal system that gives them the opportunity to discuss advancement
- Professional working conditions that are conducive to productivity and effectiveness

- Compensation that is related to their accomplishments and responsibility
- The opportunity to take normal business risks in a nonpunitive environment, without fear of excessive reprisals

Human Tendencies in Planning

There are a number of human tendencies that can interfere with or restrict the company's planning process.

- *Optimism:* The belief that performance will improve over the next few months
- *Short-term orientation:* An emphasis on quarterly and monthly goals and reviews, with the period beyond the first year deemphasized
- *Oversimplifying the environment:*
  Not anticipating competitive reactions to the company's moves
  Assuming that the past will extend into the future
  Point forecasting rather than forecasting a range of outcomes
- *Unwillingness to face tough issues:*
  Postponing corrective actions in the hope that the problem will disappear
  Devoting attention to issues that are interesting but not critical
- *Ambiguity in strategic definition:*
  Overstating cash flow expectations
  Understating capital needs
  Having inadequate strategic coordination
- *Minimizing the difficulty of change:*
  Entering new, relatively unknown marketplaces
  Not adequately planning and testing new ventures

Reasons Why People Resist Planning

There are a number of reasons why people resist the planning process:

- They have an unclear understanding of the benefits that can result.
- Planning is time-consuming.
- Planning requires intuitive thinking rather than doing.
- The process requires writing plans and sharing them with others.
- The process involves accountability; it creates an environment in which they will be measured and critiqued.
- People often define themselves by what they do rather than by how they contribute to the organization's profitability and success.

Significant Planning Guidelines and Policies

Planning guidelines and policies are statements or ground rules that provide a framework for management decisions and actions that are related to the achievement of organizational objectives.

The framework established by these guidelines and policies also affects decisions made within the context of the strategic plan. It is not concerned with day-to-day decisions as long as those decisions are consistent with strategic objectives.

This framework, in general, serves three important purposes: It (1) provides guidelines, (2) establishes limitations, and (3) focuses direction.

The framework is important for planning in a number of ways:

1. It helps to sharpen and define the organization's mission and focus.
2. It eliminates the need to make the same decisions repeatedly.
3. It ensures that efforts are not expended in areas that are not acceptable to senior management.
4. It provides measurable parameters for performance that cannot be violated without triggering a managerial response.

What follows are some examples of policies and policy statements, from a variety of corporate perspectives, that help to illus-

trate these points and can serve as models for anyone whose job
it is to create and draft policies.

Financial

*The company will reinvest at least 60 percent of its net income
in the business.*

*It is the company's objective to pay a regular dividend to com-
mon shareholders on a quarterly basis.*

Corporate Development

*The company will not enter businesses in which the market
growth rate is less than 15 percent.*

*All acquisitions of other companies, whether in whole or part,
must have the approval of the board of directors.*

*Companies will be acquired only if their markets are known
to senior management and there are synergistic benefits to
the relationship.*

*Our corporate image and purpose shall always be main-
tained. We will consider only opportunities for investment
or acquisition that will maintain or enhance our corporate
image of progressiveness, technical excellence, customer
commitment, and merchandising preeminence in the sale
of quality products and services. New opportunities will not
be considered if they will in any way compromise the reputation for being an ethical company with due regard to
human and social responsibilities that we have worked so
hard to achieve and maintain. Our employees command
respect for their business abilities, integrity, fairness, and
humanity.*

*Investment, whether capital expenditure or corporate acqui-
sition, requires a return on equity of 20 percent or greater.
This serves to enhance our current expectations for corporate performance.*

Corporate

*The company will prepare a three-year strategic plan and an
annual budget.*

The company will establish goals for each of these documents, measure the performance of its staff against these parameters, and incorporate these evaluations into its compensation plans.

It is company policy to comply with all OSHA and EPA regulations. We will develop training programs that will assure compliance without the need for outside audit. The company will make certain that employee safety is always emphasized and never compromised in all of its activities.

It is the company's policy to comply with generally accepted accounting principles in the preparation of information for any regulatory agency, financial institution, or any other interest that may receive this information.

Some Additional Issues

Budgets should be developed by those who have the responsibility for their achievement, subject to the requirements and expectations of the organization.

A budget need not be completely detailed in every respect in order to be effective and valuable. The level of detail should be governed by the value of the information being developed.

Every excellent plan is almost out of date by the time it is being used. The value of the planning process is the thinking, research, and communication that the process fosters.

The coordinator of the budget process should have considerable knowledge of the business, its products, and its markets. While accounting and finance are important areas of knowledge, developing the budget is a management challenge rather than an accounting responsibility.

A Guide to Better Budgets

- Start simple.
- Have each function and area of responsibility prepare its own budget, consistent with corporate goals, objectives, constraints, and policies.

- Recognize that effective budgets require senior management approval and the endorsement of the organization.
- Understand that having a budget improves the performance of the entire organization and each of its parts—really.
- Understand that a budget is developed to ensure that every department head is working toward the same goal, with knowledge of the department's resources and constraints.
- Recognize that the budget department does not create the budget. It is simply a coordinator, consultant, and adviser.
- Arrange educational meetings to ensure an understanding of the process and the expectations for it. Do this at least twice during the process.
- Make certain that interdepartmental relations are coordinated. Departments cannot perform well without the cooperation of other departments. Make certain that these interdependencies are properly documented.
- Ensure that expenditures above a specific threshold amount that are included in the budget are supported with proper documentation and financial analysis.
- Incorporate into the budget procedure specific requirements covering approval for nonbudgeted expenditures and cost overruns.
- To sell the budget concept, select one department or profit center manager to convey the value of developing an intelligent budget. Demonstrate how the budget has improved the performance of this manager's organization. The word will spread among the manager's peers.
- Express budget procedures in writing. Document corporate targets, policies, and constraints and convey them to everyone who is involved in the process. Update this documentation frequently.
- Provide each involved department with information on the department's past financial and statistical history, known economic factors, and the accounting chart of accounts in order to properly prepare the department for effective participation.
- Classify the expenditures of individual departments care-

fully. Do not arbitrarily allocate common costs to individual profit centers.

- Budget product and service costs on a per-unit basis if possible. Be realistic.
- Do not create theoretical models that make accountability unachievable.
- Prepare budgets that incorporate alternative environments and competitive factors. Have a fallback plan available for emergencies; identify best- and worst-case scenarios. This enhances the thought process.
- Base the sales forecast on realistic expectations. Like all other budgets, it should be achievable, but a challenge.
- Establish production plans in accordance with a detailed forecast. Incorporate purchasing and inventory strategies and product pricing expectations.
- Incorporate the cash flow improvements from the capital expenditure budget into the operating budget. These are interrelated parts of the planning process.
- Develop and share the positive and negative elements of past budget efforts into the current process. Learn from both the successes and the mistakes.
- Make sure that reports of actual performance are provided to responsibility centers in a timely manner, with the appropriate level of detail.
- Never forget that a budget and its forecast components are estimates. Precision does not count.
- Improve the quality and effectiveness of the process continuously. Make sure that everyone knows that you are focusing on this issue. Solicit and accept feedback from participants.

Preparation of the Budget

Sales Planning

Consider the historical patterns of behavior for your customers, your markets, your products, and your competitors. The success of your company depends on the success of your customers.

Company sales will be affected by the economy. Identify how future economic events will affect your business. This includes looking at consumer outlook, inflation, taxes, political events, and the business cycle.

Ask the sales organization for its input. The salespeople know the customers and markets better than anyone else. Salespeople are optimistic, by their stereotypical nature. On the other hand, they have been known to "low-ball" forecasts in order to minimize quotas. Somehow, given the balance between these two forces, a consensus forecast by the sales team usually provides very usable information.

Identify all known or anticipated events that will affect your market in the upcoming year. This should include competitors entering or leaving the market and product additions and eliminations. Industry trade shows are an excellent source of this information: Look at what is and what is not being featured. What shows companies take booths at is often an indicator of those companies' perceived strategic identity.

The sales and marketing teams should identify the level of customer service that is necessary if the company is to achieve a competitive advantage. Strategies involving inventory and the entire supply chain should be based upon customer service expectations.

Operations Planning

Capacity should be defined based upon the expected product mix. This will provide insights into pricing decisions and decisions as to whether to pursue marginal business.

Product mix capability and flexibility are very important. How rapidly machinery can be changed between products will provide guidance for determining required minimum orders and the extent to which discounts should be offered for very large orders.

The company should consider the number of shifts to be operated. This depends on both the relative efficiency of each shift and the size of an ideal production run. If machine change-over is expensive, working four 10- or 12-hour shifts will be more cost-effective than working five 8-hour days. Overtime can be built into the schedule.

Technology can make a major contribution to improving the efficiency of the overall operation. Establishing computerized hookups among customer orders, machine and workforce schedules, and raw material logistics will:

- Improve customer service
- Accelerate billing and cash flow
- Reduce work-in-process inventory and time
- Reduce raw materials inventory
- Usually pay for itself in less than a year

The capital budget can be prepared after all of the previously mentioned analyses have been performed. Return on investment analysis and the capital budget are discussed at some length in Chapter 10.

You should consider outsourcing less important resource-consuming operations. This will free up assets, cash, and people for more important activities.

Chapter 13

Selected Business Readings

THIS CHAPTER CONTAINS THREE ARTICLES dealing with themes that are appropriate for this book for several reasons:

1. They advocate management thinking that can be characterized as:
   - Contrarian
   - "Out of the box"
   - Nontraditional

   Many companies are managed from an accounting-oriented perspective. There are certain approaches, such as conservatism and being risk averse, that are appropriate for the accounting department but may be less so for other areas. In those areas, "out of the box," nontraditional management styles are often desirable and necessary. Many of the techniques of financial analysis that are described in this book support the more contrarian corporate strategies.

2. These articles tie in with the planning and budget process described in Chapter 12. They discuss a number of issues that surface during the development of the budget. While Chapter 12 describes many practices that make the process work successfully in corporations, these articles identify in greater analytical detail what the outcomes of the budget process should be.

"Profitability During Tough Times" offers some insights into how to thrive in a highly competitive environment. It advocates contrarian thinking and strategy development and offers some specific insights into how to focus on the real issues and break out of the traditional mold.

"Do the Right Thing" recognizes that companies sometimes need to retrench on expenses and redirect their focus. It suggests some specific actions that companies can take that will enable them to successfully respond to difficult periods without damaging the core competencies of the organization.

"Recession = Opportunity" focuses specifically on positive actions that companies should take when the psychological tone of the economy turns negative. The pressure to go along with the traditional responses is enormous. Resisting this pressure, however, can be very profitable.

Profitability During Tough Times

Many of the strategies that were appropriate and effective in the past are no longer above reproach. In fact, we have learned over the years that the global marketplace is a dynamic place, full of turmoil; therefore, rethinking of past assumptions and engaging in out-of-the-box thinking is always required. Organizations need to address this constant change, focus on the state of the world, both as it exists now and as it may be in the future, and raise their performance to new levels of effort and achievement.

Recent Progress

Product quality is no longer an issue. It is almost impossible to justify a multilevel pricing structure by offering different levels of product quality. Market segmentation now focuses on differences in features and support. Differences in product performance are acceptable. Differences in performance quality are not.

Responsive Service

You will gain competitive and profit advantages by compressing the supply chain from your suppliers to your company to your customers. The amount of time required for this sequence of events has a substantial effect on your inventory, accounts receivable, profitability, and ultimately cash flow. Service levels are affected as well, which may in turn affect your market share and sales growth.

Competitive Pricing

In many cases, competitive pricing means price reductions. This era of pricing pressure is not going to change any time soon. Asking the customer to pay for our inefficiencies is not an option. Many industries are experiencing price deflation and will continue to do so. This means that companies must find new ways to maintain their profit margins. The successful ones will become more efficient, find more value-added features to add to the product, and focus on new markets and distribution channels in order to remain competitive. Have you priced out a personal computer lately?

Companies will need to make a great effort to distinguish themselves from their competition. The new realities include very low interest rates, economic turmoil in Asia, essentially zero inflation, and a single global economy. However, a company's profitability can be enhanced, even during tough times. These realities can serve as a competitive advantage if you refocus the attention of the organization on the fundamental realities of successful business:

1. Why are we special?
2. Why do we deserve to exist?
3. Why should customers buy our products?
4. Why do we deserve to have our customers' money?

Attitudes and Strategies for Success

We exist to help *our* customers sell *their* products to *their* customers at a significant profit to both of us. This is called *strategic partnering*.

We need to help our customers solve problems and to focus

on their opportunities rather than merely providing products. Anyone can sell products. This is called *consultative selling.*

Our prosperity is enhanced as we improve our customers' ability to compete in their marketplace.

We know enough about our *customers'* businesses and markets so that we can provide products and ideas that will make our customers special.

Our people know no limits to their efforts.

Specific Action Strategies

The fundamental ingredients have not changed; only the environment in which we need to make things happen is different. Not only is thinking out of the box necessary, but I am no longer certain that there are many "boxes" remaining. Here are some strategies that are available to you:

Invest in sales professionals and their training and support. High-quality marketplace visibility is the most profitable investment your company can make.

Accelerate the development of innovative products and services. Focus your company's resources, both people and money, on those products and services that offer the opportunity for significant financial reward. Persistence is valuable—but not when it implies refusing to change direction when success is not available if you go on as you are.

Learn more about the current economic environment and the persistent global turmoil. How can you benefit? This has implications for both buying and selling. Change is good because it creates opportunities for those who are prepared and ready to take action.

Expand your marketplace support to include participation in trade shows and industry showcases, advertising in well-directed journals, and use of other media to communicate with existing and potential customers. Keep your customers aware of your constantly improving capabilities. If you have nothing new to say to your customers, your competitors will.

Streamline the performance of your administrative support.
Use technology in ways that let you derive its maximum
value. Use experts to fill in and eliminate the knowledge
gaps in your organization.

Do the Right Thing

Companies have worked hard at restructuring themselves in response to the dramatic changes that have occurred in the economy and in their marketplaces in recent years. Here are a few
thoughts concerning some of the serious errors companies have
committed in their efforts to change:

Mistake 1: Laying Off Only Lower-Level Support Staff

Personnel decisions are made by senior and middle management—who, of course, are not going to choose themselves for
outplacement. As a result, the company ends up with many
"chiefs" but not enough "Indians." Six-figure executives spend
their time typing, photocopying, and faxing when they should be
meeting with customers and planning strategies.

Executives should prioritize entire programs, products, and
markets according to profitability and opportunity. Maintaining
or even increasing the number of support staff and expanding
their responsibilities makes more time available to executives to
develop the business. Leave the more routine tasks to those who
are best trained (and appropriately paid) to perform them.

Mistake 2: Seeing the Future as an Extension of the Past.

During times of marketplace turmoil and uncertainty, some
companies seek out those programs, strategies, and attitudes
that worked well in the past. This provides a level of organizational comfort and eases the tensions associated with change.
However, sticking to what has always worked well may, in fact,
be perpetuating approaches that are no longer valid as a result of
new market conditions.

There should be no sacred cows when the company underachieves. Reexamine and reprioritize all of the company's operations and activities.

Mistake 3: Not Recycling Past Ideas That Merit Current Consideration

Whether an idea is profitable or not depends on both the timing of its implementation and the management support it receives. Something that did not work seven years ago may have considerable merit now.

The market may currently need some products and services that it did not need in the past. List, explore, and give consideration to all ideas. With input from everyone concerned, make a list of *all* possible courses of action. Some resurrected fundamentals or past failures may in fact save the day.

Mistake 4: Reducing Price Rather Than Adding Value

Giving the customer a price discount may result in a sale. It can also encourage the customer either to expect further discounts in the future or to ask, "If you can afford to reduce the price now, does that mean that you were gouging me in the past?"

Your objective is to create a loyal market, not merely to make a sale. Pressures to reduce the price are lessened when you add value to the sale. Value-added features could include:

- Faster delivery
- Higher quality
- Educating customers on product applications
- User conferences
- Focus groups for product improvement
- Improved customer service

These activities enhance your competitive position.

Getting a new customer is very difficult. Keeping an existing customer happy is a great challenge. Getting back a customer that you have already lost is almost impossible.

Mistake 5: Ignoring the 80 Percent/20 Percent Rule

You need to realize that 20 percent of your customers account for 80 percent of your revenue, and 20 percent of your products result in 80 percent of your shipments. Less positively, 20 percent of your employees account for 80 percent of your absenteeism, and 20 percent of your customers are responsible for 80 percent of your overdue accounts receivable.

Companies confuse activity with productivity and productivity with effectiveness. They try to be all things to all people. Every order receives fanatical attention from exhausted, overworked people who hope and believe that if they can just work harder, things will improve. Focus your energies on the activities that are most important. The least important 80 percent of all corporate activity results in only 20 percent of the achievement. Do not dilute the effort and compromise the performance of the most important tasks by expending too much energy on that least important 80 percent. Intelligent corporate prioritizing and time management ensures that the most important work gets done.

Achievement = Productivity = Effectiveness = Profitability

Mistake 6: Holding On to Sacred Cows

The entire business should be evaluated periodically, perhaps at budget time. Is each of the product lines and markets still providing its expected contribution? Is any product line or market consuming an inordinate share of corporate resources, beyond what is justified by present and expected future performance? What other, more profitable ventures can be implemented with underproductive resources? Should we really be in this business?

Recession = Opportunity

There is a lot of talk these days about how this period of prosperity cannot last forever. This is certainly a true statement, because nothing lasts forever. The fact is that many public companies have already begun to report reduced earnings. There are many explanations for this.

1. Companies that sell to Asia or Europe have already been experiencing a recession. Those with heavy investments in the Far East have certainly been having severe problems for the past few years. The Japanese stock market is down over 60 percent from its highs in the early 1990s. The strong American dollar (until recently) has forced U.S.-based exporters to make difficult choices concerning market share and profitability. The issue facing many is, given the price pressures, should they sell at reduced margins and keep the business, or is selling at low margins not worth the effort?

2. The absence of inflation on a global scale has helped some companies, but hurt others. Oil drilling companies and companies in other businesses involving the production of commodities have been in a significant recession for quite some time. Some agriculturally based businesses have been so successful at improving productivity that they have excess capacity and their production is far above what the market needs.

3. Overbuilding of capacity in some very capital-intensive industries has resulted in a Darwinian selection process among competitors. It is very difficult for these companies to adjust to weak demand and rapid technological change.

4. Companies that have a relatively fixed way of doing business have been unable or slow to respond to the new methods of doing business that have come about because of technological changes. These new business models have affected the supply chain and attitudes about outsourcing, and have redefined or actually created a relationship between the original supplier and the ultimate customer.

5. Disintermediation has drastically affected all supplier/customer relationships. An intermediary is a middleman, someone who is in between. A traditional wholesaler or distributor buys from the manufacturer and sells to the

retailer, who in turn sells to the consumer. A retail store is an example of an intermediary. Sometimes the intermediary's only contribution to the process is buying in large quantities and being willing to sell in smaller quantities. In effect, these intermediaries are inventory managers who provide extended credit terms.

Technology is permitting a direct relationship between the manufacturer and the customer. We can buy cars and airline tickets on the Internet, and we can trade stocks and bonds as well. We used to get all of these things through intermediaries—car dealers, travel agents, and stockbrokers. The reduction in the role and value of these intermediaries is called *disintermediation.*

Action Plans for Success

So the question that arises is, "What happens if there is a recession? How will it affect the company, and what should we do?"

1. Don't panic or overreact. Think strategically, with perspective. Across-the-board expense reductions are usually counterproductive. They penalize the most efficient departments, result in higher-level people doing less productive work, and exacerbate the problem of keeping your focus on the most profitable place for your investment dollars.
2. Refocus on your customers. What do they want from you, what do they expect of you, and why do they buy from you? What is the real value that you offer? Examine how technology will enable you to reposition yourself in the supply chain. Help your customers lower their inventory and reduce delivery times.
3. Enhance your marketing efforts. The best opportunity to gain market share is when your competitors are reducing their sales forces, trade show appearances, advertising, and promotional efforts. Potential customers are more willing to consider a change, and your competitors' presence is being reduced.
4. Identify and pursue new applications for your organiza-

tion's skills and capabilities. There are many companies out there that are not perceived as traditional customers for your industry. Go after them. You may be the only one who will. Change is an almost universally accepted fact of life these days, and any organization that resists change will fail. We are all someone else's outsource. What kind of businesses would consider your products or services valuable?

Who are your competitors? They may not all be companies that look like yours. The list of competitors may be changing constantly as companies and supply chains are redefined. Competition is defined by contribution and value added, not by the physical appearance of those who compete. The biggest threat to Barnes & Noble bookstores is Amazon.com. This is a classic concept called *marketing myopia* that was first identified many years ago by Theodore Levitt of the Harvard Business School.

5. Collect those receivables. Enhance your cash flow. This is everyone's responsibility. The faster the money comes in, the more money you will have available, sooner, for reinvestment. Sell off underperforming assets, including inventory, fixed assets, and products, to raise and redirect cash flow.

6. Have your management team do a S.W.O.T. analysis. This is an incredibly valuable corporate self-assessment of where in the global economy your company currently is and where it needs to be. S.W.O.T. stands for *s*trengths, *w*eaknesses, *o*pportunities and *t*hreats. Such an analysis enables the company to identify and focus on all of the positive and negative issues that need to be dealt with. This should be an annual effort that precedes budget preparation. Refer back to Chapter 12 for more discussion on this.

Strategic Issues and the Global Economy

Our domestic economy has not experienced any noteworthy inflation for quite a few years. The inflation indexes—the consumer price index (CPI) and the producer price index (PPI)—are statistical averages that reflect real economic events. However, they also tend to mask divergent trends that the casual observer may not detect, but that in fact have considerable impact on certain sectors of our economy. The prime example here is the serious decline in the price of oil, and its reversal again more recently.

As a result of the strength of our domestic economy, the dollar has been very strong relative to other currencies. As a result, imports have become less expensive. However, our competitive position globally is subject to very inflexible price ceilings. If the dollar weakens, the impact on the statistical averages, and also on the domestic economy, will be very bearish.

Imports will become relatively more expensive. The higher levels of inflation shown by the indexes might cause the Federal Reserve to increase interest rates, leading to a much lower stock market, declining individual net worth, less consumer spending, and more business caution—in other words, a recession.

Incredible technological advances in information, manufacturing, and agriculture have improved our productive capacity and the efficiencies of our business practices to an extraordinary degree. Technology, corporate ambition, and competitive pressures have caused the business relationships in which our company is involved—its sources of supply and its customers—to be truly global. To be successful, we must revisit the fundamental, age-old business questions: How do we add value to our customers? How well do we serve them? How efficiently and effectively does our company perform?

Appendix A

Financial Statement Practice

Middlesex Manufacturing Company

The following list gives all the financial categories of Middlesex Manufacturing Company, Inc. For each item in the list, identify whether it belongs on the balance sheet or the income statement and write the number in the correct places. Correctly placing the numbers will provide you with an excellent review of the structure and content of the financial statements.

Corporate Income Tax Expense	$	2,000
Accounts Receivable		3,000
Telephone Expense		7,000
Cost of Goods Sold		140,000
Wages Expense		29,000
Total Current Assets		12,000
Advertising Expense		10,000
Inventory, End of Year		7,000
Net Other Income/(Expense)		(1,000)
Beginning Balance, Retained Earnings		5,000
Dividends		2,000
Accounts Payable		6,000
Gross Profit		30%
Accumulated Depreciation		14,000
Buildings		50,000
Cash		2,000

Depreciation Expense	5,000
Total Operating Expenses	51,000
Common Stock	26,000
Purchases, Net	138,000
Inventory, Beginning of Year	9,000
Total Stockholders' Equity	35,000
Machinery & Equipment	12,000
Ending Balance, Retained Earnings	9,000
Mortgage Payable	19,000
Revenue	200,000

Middlesex Manufacturing Company, Inc.
Balance Sheet

Assets

Current Assets

* ....

* ....

* ....

Total Current Assets $_____

Fixed Assets

* ....

^ ....

* .... (.................)... _____

Net Fixed Assets $_____

Total Assets .... $_____

Liabilities & Stockholders Equity

Current Liabilities

* ....

* ....

Total Current Liabilities .... $_____

Long Term Debt .... _____

Total Liabilities .... $_____

Stockholders' Equity

* ....

* ....

* ....

Total Stockholders' Equity .... _____

Total Liabilities & Stockholders' Equity .... $_____

Middlesex Manufacturing Company, Inc.
Income Statement

Revenue .... $ 100%

Cost of Goods Sold Calculation
     Beginning Inventory ....
    + Purchases ....
    = Goods Available For Sale ....
    − Ending Inventory ....

= Cost of Goods Sold .... $ %

Gross Profit .... $ 30%

Operating Expenses
* ....
* ....
* ....
* ....

Total Operating Expenses .... $

Income From Operations .... $

Net Other Income (Expense) .... $

Net Income Before Tax .... $

Corporate Income Tax Expense .... $

Net Income (Loss) .... $

Statement of Retained Earnings

Beginning Balance, Retained Earnings ..... $

+ Net Income (Loss) ....

− Dividends ....

= Ending Balance, Retained Earnings ..... $

Appendix A Answer Key

Middlesex Manufacturing Company, Inc.
Balance Sheet

Assets

Current Assets

*..........Cash	$ 2,000...	
*..........Accounts Receivable	3,000...	
*..........Inventory	7,000...	
Total Current Assets		$12,000

Fixed Assets

*..........Furniture and Equipment	$12,000...	
*..........Buildings	50,000...	
*..........Accumulated Depreciation	.. (..14,000)...	
Net Fixed Assets		$48,000
Total Assets		$60,000

Liabilities & Stockholders Equity

Current Liabilities

*.....Accounts Payable	$ 6,000...	
*		
Total Current Liabilities		$ 6,000
Long-Term Debt		$19,000
Total Liabilities		$25,000

Stockholders' Equity

*.....Retained Earnings	$ 9,000...	
*.....Common Stock	26,000...	
....		
Total Stockholders' Equity		$35,000
Total Liabilities and Stockholders' Equity .		$60,000

Middlesex Manufacturing Company, Inc.
Income Statement

Revenue		$200,000	100%
Cost of Goods Sold Calculation			
Beginning Inventory	$ 9,000...		
+ Purchases	+ 138,000...		
= Goods Available for Sale	= 147,000...		
− Ending Inventory	− 7,000...		
= **Cost of Goods Sold**		140,000	70%
Gross Profit		$ 60,000	30%
Operating Expenses			
*.....Telephone	$ 7,000...		
*.....Wages	29,000...		
*,,,,,Advertising	10,000...		
*.....Depreciation	5,000...		
Total Operating Expenses		51,000	
Income From Operations		$ 9,000	
Net Other Income (Expense)		(1,000)	
Net Income Before Tax		$ 8,000	
Corporate Income Tax Expense		2,000	
Net Income (Loss)		$ 6,000	

Statement of Retained Earnings

Beginning Balance, Retained Earnings	$	5,000
+ Net Income (Loss)	+	6,000
− Dividends	−	2,000
= Ending Balance, Retained Earnings	$	9,000

Appendix B

Matching Exercise

Match the definitions at the right with the terms they best describe.

Select 70 of these.

Assets _____ 2

Accounting _____

Accounts payables _____

Accrual Accounting _____

AICPA _____

Balance Sheet _____

Breakeven _____

Budget _____

Cash Flow _____

CPA _____

CFO _____

Collateral _____

Corporation _____

1. Borrow with collateral
2. What the company owns
3. The value of an asset at disposal
4. A measure of receivable collection
5. Costs that do not change with production volume
6. Debt due within a year
7. An option to buy
8. A vehicle for investing
9. Laws that protect investors
10. Reporting the past in dollars
11. Important
12. A ratio that measures efficiency
13. Where stocks are traded

Bond _____

14. An option to buy commodities

Current Liabilities _____

15. What the company owes vendors

Debentures _____

16. Expenses paid before the time period that will benefit

Depreciation _____

17. A company owned by another company

Dividend _____

18. Corporate executive who manages cash

Stockholders' Equity _____

19. A bond contract

Fiscal year _____

20. A review of a company's books

Fixed costs _____

21. An independent market maker

Goodwill _____

22. The price a buyer is willing to pay

Interest ___ _____

23. Trading securities by computer

Inventory _____

24. Recording revenues when earned

Expense _____

25. Accounting year

Leverage _____

26. Profits kept within the company

LIFO _____

27. A representative of a lending organization

Liquid _____

28. Portion of profits paid to the federal government

Material _____

29. An option to sell

Mortgage _____

30. Accountants' professional association

Prepaid expenses _____

31. Statement of financial position

Retained earnings _____

32. The point at which revenues = expenses

Sinking fund _____

33. The premium over fair market value paid for an acquisition

Variable costs _____

34. A documentation of the financial planning process

Revenue _____

35. The fee paid to a lender for a loan

Ratio _____

36. Funds set aside to pay debt

IRS _____

37. Costs that fluctuate with production volume

Controller _____ *43*

38. A person who helps you buy stock

Direct _____

39. A liquidity ratio

Subsidiary _____ *17*

40. Comparing the performance of competitors

Salvage value _____

41. Borrowing money to buy securities

Profitability ratios _____

42. Selling stock not currently owned

FIFO _____ *95*   *∅*

43. A company's chief accountant

EBIT _____ *64*

44. Ratios to measure performance

Benchmarking _____

45. Agent who helps buyers and sellers

Quick ratio _____

46. The price at which a seller will sell

13D _____

47. A security offering announcement

Turnover _____

48. A group of investors

Days' Sales Outstan

49. Net income + depreciation

Treasurer _____

50. Certified Public Accountant

Banker _____ *27*

51. Chief Financial Officer

Stockbroker _____ *76*

52. The annual report to the SEC

Mutual Fund _____

Stock Exchange _____

Indenture _____

Audit _____

Taxes _____ 2B

Stockholders _____ 59

Investors _____

10K _____

Greenmail _____

Tender _____

Proxy _____ 61

Liquidator _____

Prospectus _____ 70

IPO _____ 57

Syndicate _____

Tombstone _____

Blue Sky laws _____

Specialist _____

Bid _____ 22

Asked _____

53. Assets pledged as security for a loan

54. Labor and material are costs

55. First-in, first-out; an inventory accounting method

56. Easily convertible to cash

57. A company's initial sale of stock to the public

58. An offer to buy stock

59. The owners of the corporation

60. Larry is one of these

61. A way of voting stock

62. An accounting entity

63. Allocation that reduces an asset's book value

64. Earnings before interest and taxes

65. A distribution of net income to owners of a corporation

66. A mathematical comparison of two or more numbers; used to evaluate performance

67. The entity you pay taxes to

68. Dollar amount of products or services a company provides to customers

69. Last-in, first-out; an inventory accounting method

70. Document describing the terms of a stock offering

71. The use of borrowed money to expand a business

72. Products being manufactured or available for sale

Broker _____   73. Cost of operating the busi-
                                   ness

Short Sale _____   74. Buying out an undesirable in-
                                   vestor

Margin _____   75. SEC takeover filing

Program trading _____   76. People who buy stocks and
                                   bonds

Future _____   77. Shareholders' ownership po-
                                   sition

Call _____   78. A form of corporate debt

Put _____   79. Bonds that are not secured by
                                   specific collateral

Appendix B Answer Key

Match the definitions at the right with the terms they best describe.

Select 70 of these.

Assets ___2___	1.	Borrow with collateral
Accounting ___10___	2.	What the company owns
Accounts payables ___15___	3.	The value of an asset at disposal
Accrual Accounting ___24___	4.	A measure of receivable collection
AICPA ___30___	5.	Costs that do not change with production volume
Balance Sheet ___31___	6.	Debt due within a year
Breakeven ___32___	7.	An option to buy
Budget ___34___	8.	A vehicle for investing
Cash Flow ___49___	9.	Laws that protect investors
CPA ___50___	10.	Reporting the past in dollars
CFO ___51___	11.	Important
Collateral ___53___	12.	A ratio that measures efficiency
Corporation ___62___	13.	Where stocks are traded

Bond _____78_____   14. An option to buy commodi-
                                     ties

Current Liabilities __6__   15. What the company owes ven-
                                     dors

Debentures __79__   16. Expenses paid before the
                                     time period that will benefit

Depreciation __63__   17. A company owned by an-
                                     other company

Dividend __65__   18. Corporate executive who
                                     manages cash

Stockholders' Equity __77__   19. A bond contract
Fiscal year __25__   20. A review of a company's
                                     books

Fixed costs __5__   21. An independent market
                                     maker

Goodwill __33__   22. The price a buyer is willing to
                                     pay

Interest __35__   23. Trading securities by com-
                                     puter

Inventory __72__   24. Recording revenues when
                                     earned

Expense __73__   25. Accounting year
Leverage __71__   26. Profits kept within the com-
                                     pany

LIFO __69__   27. A representative of a lending
                                     organization

Liquid __56__   28. Portion of profits paid to the
                                     federal government

Material __11__   29. An option to sell
Mortgage __1__   30. Accountants' professional as-
                                     sociation

Prepaid expenses __16__   31. Statement of financial posi-
                                     tion

Retained earnings __26__   32. The point at which revenues
                                     = expenses

Sinking fund ____36____

Variable costs ____37____

Revenue ____68____

Ratio ____66____

IRS ____67____

Controller ____43____

Direct ____54____

Subsidiary ____17____

Salvage value ____3____

Profitability ratios ____44____

FIFO ____55____

EBIT ____64____

Benchmarking ____40____

Quick ratio ____39____

13D ____75____

Turnover ____12____

Days' Sales Outstanding ____4____

Treasurer ____18____

Banker ____27____

Stockbroker ____38____

33. The premium over fair market value paid for an acquisition

34. A documentation of the financial planning process

35. The fee paid to a lender for a loan

36. Funds set aside to pay debt

37. Costs that fluctuate with production volume

38. A person who helps you buy stock

39. A liquidity ratio

40. Comparing the performance of competitors

41. Borrowing money to buy securities

42. Selling stock not currently owned

43. A company's chief accountant

44. Ratios to measure performance

45. Agent who helps buyers and sellers

46. The price at which a seller will sell

47. A security offering announcement

48. A group of investors

49. Net income + depreciation

50. Certified Public Accountant

51. Chief Financial Officer

52. The annual report to the SEC

Mutual Fund ____8____   53. Assets pledged as security for a loan

Stock Exchange ____13____   54. Labor and material are costs

Indenture ____19____   55. First-in, first-out; an inventory accounting method

Audit ____20____   56. Easily convertible to cash

Taxes ____28____   57. A company's initial sale of stock to the public

Stockholders ____59____   58. An offer to buy stock

Investors ____76____   59. The owners of the corporation

10K ____52____   60. Larry is one of these

Greenmail ____74____   61. A way of voting stock

Tender ____58____   62. An accounting entity

Proxy ____61____   63. Allocation that reduces an asset's book value

Liquidator ____60____   64. Earnings before interest and taxes

Prospectus ____70____   65. A distribution of net income to owners of a corporation

IPO ____57____   66. A mathematical comparison of two or more numbers; used to evaluate performance

Syndicate ____48____   67. The entity you pay taxes to

Tombstone ____47____   68. Dollar amount of products or services a company provides to customers

Blue Sky laws ____9____   69. Last-in, first-out; an inventory accounting method

Specialist ____21____   70. Document describing the terms of a stock offering

Bid ____22____   71. The use of borrowed money to expand a business

Asked ____46____   72. Products being manufactured or available for sale

Broker _____45_____ 73. Cost of operating the business

Short Sale _____42_____ 74. Buying out an undesirable investor

Margin _____41_____ 75. SEC takeover filing

Program trading _____23_____ 76. People who buy stocks and bonds

Future _____14_____ 77. Shareholders' ownership position

Call _____7_____ 78. A form of corporate debt

Put _____29_____ 79. Bonds that are not secured by specific collateral

Appendix C

PALEY PRODUCTS

Robert Eng, vice president and loan officer of the First National Bank of Chicago, Illinois, was recently alerted to the deteriorating financial position of one of its clients, Paley Products, by the bank's newly installed computerized loan analysis program. The bank requires quarterly financial statements (balance sheet, income statement, and sources and uses of funds) from each of its loan customers. The data from the financial statements are entered into a spreadsheet program that calculates the key ratios, charts trends, and compares the ratios and trends with those of other firms in the same industry. If any of the company's ratios are significantly inferior to the industry average, the computer produces an exception report and highlights the problem. If the terms of the loan agreement require either that certain levels of assets be maintained or that a minimum of certain ratios be achieved, the output report will identify deficiencies.

Paley Products is a manufacturer of a full line of computer components. In addition to its regular products, Paley markets special lines of products for both the home and school markets, some of which are also appropriate for seasonal gift items. Its working capital needs have been financed primarily through loans from First National Bank, which has provided Paley Products with a line of credit amounting to $300,000. In accordance with common banking practices, the line of credit agreement provides that the loan be paid in full each July.

The first financial analysis of Paley Products had revealed a downward trend in certain performance ratios, below what was deemed acceptable for the component manufacturing industry as reflected by the industry averages, although no specific ratio that was identified in the loan agreement was in violation. However, subsequent analyses continued to reflect this downward trend. Mr. Eng had previously discussed his concern with Frank Paley, president of Palcy Products, but no corrective action appeared to have been taken. The latest analysis showed the current ratio below the required 2.0 specified in the loan agreement. This conclusion was based on the financial information contained in Exhibits C-1, C-2, and C-3. According to provisions in the loan agreement, First National Bank could call the loan at any time after the ratio requirements had been violated. The company would then have ten days to correct the problem, pay off the loan, or face foreclosure proceedings. The day of reckoning had arrived. While Mr. Eng had no intention of actually enforcing the contract to its fullest at this time, he did intend to use the provisions of the loan agreement to get Mr. Paley to take some decisive actions over the coming months to improve the company's financial picture.

Exhibit C-1. Paley Products, Inc. Income Statements for the Years Ending December 31,

	1999	2000	2001
Revenue	$2,652,000	$2,754,000	$2,856,000
Cost of Goods Sold	2,121,600	2,203,200	2,284,800
Gross Profit	$ 530,400	$ 550,800	$ 571,200
General and Adminstrative			
Expenses	$ 204,000	$ 224,400	$ 244,800
Depreciation	81,600	102,000	122,400
Miscellaneous	40,800	85,700	122,400
Net Income Before Taxes	$ 204,000	$ 138,700	$ 81,600
Income Taxes @ 35%	71,400	48,545	28,560
Net Income	$ 132,600	$ 90,155	$ 53,040

Exhibit C-2. Computer Component Manufacturing Industry Financial Ratios, 2001

Quick Ratio	1.0
Current Ratio	2.7
Inventory Turnover	7.0
Average Collection Period	32 days
Total Asset Turnover	2.6×
Fixed Asset Turnover	13.0×
Return on Assets	11.7%
Return on Net Worth	23.4%
Debt Ratio	50.0%
Profit Margin on Sales	4.5%

Industry averages have been constant during this time period. These numbers are based on year-end amounts.

Higher costs, especially increases in the costs of certain out-sourced materials and in the wages of highly skilled technicians, have led to a decline in Paley Products' margins over the years. Sales increased during this time period because of aggressive marketing programs. Competition within various segments of the computer industry is continuing to grow more intense, both technologically and financially.

Mr. Paley received a copy of the latest analysis from the bank, along with a blunt statement that the bank would insist on complete retirement of the loan unless corrective actions were implemented. Although he did not totally agree with the bank's assessment of his company's financial condition and was not fully certain of what his future course should be, Mr. Paley began to develop a "recovery" plan. He immediately concluded that sales growth could not continue without an increase in the bank line of credit from the current $300,000 to $400,000. Also, a progress payment of $100,000 for construction in progress was due the following year. Mr. Paley felt a sense of urgency despite the fact that his relationship with First National Bank of Chicago had begun many years earlier.

The ratio calculations that the bank used are given in Exhibit C-4. Calculate each of the ratios and think about the performance concerns that these trends reflect.

Exhibit C-3. Paley Products, Inc. Comparative Balance Sheets, December 31,

	1999	2000	2001
Cash	$ 61,000	$ 28,600	$ 20,400
Accounts Receivable	245,000	277,400	388,000
Inventory	306,000	510,000	826,200
Current Assets	$612,000	$ 816,000	$1,234,600
Gross Book Value	$600,000	$ 730,500	$ 826,300
Accumulated Depreciation	(371,400)	(473,400)	(595,800)
Net Book Values:			
Land and Building	49,000	130,600	122,400
Machinery	151,000	118,300	102,000
Other Fixed Assets	28,600	8,200	6,100
Total Assets	$840,600	$1,073,100	$1,465,100
Bank Notes Payable	$ —	$ 102,000	$ 286,000
Accounts Payable	98,000	155,000	306,000
Accruals	49,000	57,000	77,500
Current Liabilities	$147,000	$ 314,000	$ 669,500
Mortgage	45,000	40,800	36,700
Common Stock	365,000	365,000	365,000
Retained Earnings	283,600	353,300	393,900
Liabilities + Equity	$840,600	$1,073,100	$1,465,100

Phase 2

Here is Mr. Paley's proposed improvement program:

PALEY PRODUCTS, INC
PROFIT IMPROVEMENT PROGRAM, 2002

Revenue: +3% growth
Gross margin: 20%
Expenses: Same amounts as prior year
Days' sales outstanding: Improve to 40 days

Exhibit C-4. Paley Products, Inc. Ratio Calculations

$$\text{Current Ratio} = \frac{\text{Current Assets}}{\text{Current Liabilities}}$$

$$\text{Quick Ratio} = \frac{\text{Current Assets} - \text{Inventory}}{\text{Current Liabilities}}$$

$$\text{Inventory Turnover} = \frac{\text{Cost of Goods Sold}}{\text{Inventory}}$$

$$\text{Collection Period} = \frac{\text{Accounts Receivable}}{\text{Annual Revenue}/365 = \text{Average Revenue per Day}}$$

$$\text{Asset Turnover} = \frac{\text{Annual Revenue}}{\text{Total Assets}}$$

$$\text{Fixed Asset Turnover} = \frac{\text{Annual Revenue}}{\text{Fixed Assets}}$$

$$\text{Return on Assets} = \frac{\text{Net Income}}{\text{Total Assets}}$$

$$\text{Return on Net Worth} = \frac{\text{Net Income}}{\text{Net Worth (Equity)}}$$

$$\text{Debt Ratio} = \frac{\text{Total Debt}}{\text{Total Assets}}$$

$$\text{Profit Margin on Sales} = \frac{\text{Net Income}}{\text{Annual Revenue}}$$

Inventory turnover: Improve to 4
Capital expenditures: $100,000
Dividends: None until bank debt is retired
Accruals/mortgage/accounts payable: Same amounts; no changes

He was not sure what bank debt payments he could make, or how much debt he could retire, nor was he sure what his cash position would be.

Forecast the income statement, balance sheet, and sources and uses of funds statement for Paley Products. Will the company be able to pay off any of its debt?

Appendix C Answer Key

Paley Products, Inc.
Phase 1: Calculation of Ratios

	Industry Average	Paley Products		
		2001	2000	1999
Quick Ratio	1.0	0.61	1.0	2.1
Current Ratio	2.7	1.8	2.6	4.2
Inventory Turnover	7.0x	2.8x	4.3x	6.9x
Average Collection Period (Days)	32	50	37	34
Total Asset Turnover	2.6x	1.9x	2.6x	3.2x
Fixed Asset Turnover	13.0 x	12.4 x	10.7 x	11.6 x
Return on Assets	11.7%	3.6%	8.4%	15.8%
Debt Ratio	50%	48%	33%	22%
Return on Sales	4.5%	1.8%	3.3%	5.1%
Return on Net Worth (Equity)	23.4%	7.0%	12.0%	20.0%

What issues are faced by Paley Products, as evidenced by these answers. Are they problems of the company? Of the industry? Both?

A Sources and Uses of Funds Statement for the past year is provided as reference.

Paley Products, Inc.
Sources and Uses of Funds
2001

Sources of Funds		Uses of Funds	
Net Income	$ 53,040	Increase in Accounts Receivable	$110,600
Depreciation	122,400	Increase in Inventory	316,200
Increase in Bank Notes	184,000	Capital Expenditures	95,800
Increase in Accounts Payable	151,000	Decrease in Mortgage	4,100
Increase in Accruals	20,500	Dividends	12,440
Total Sources	$530,940	Total Uses	$539,140
Decrease in Cash Balance			$ 8,200

Answers Phase 2

Paley Products, Inc.
Forecast Income Statement, 2002

	Actual 2001	Forecast 2002	
Revenue	$2,856,000	$2,941,680	+3%
Cost of Goods Sold	2,284,800	2,353,344	
Gross Profit	$ 571,200	$ 588,336	20% gross profit
General and Administrative Expenses	$ 244,800	$ 244,800	Same
Depreciation	122,400	122,400	Same
Miscellaneous	122,400	122,400	Same
Net Income Before Taxes	$ 81,600	$ 98,736	
Income Taxes @ 35%	28,560	34,558	
Net Income	$ 53,040	$ 64,178	

Paley Products, Inc.
Forecast Balance Sheet

	Actual 2001	Forecast 2002
Cash	$ 20,400	$ 124,466
Accounts Receivable	388,000	322,376
Inventory	826,200	588,336
Current Assets	$1,234,600	$1,035,178
Gross Book Value	$826,300	$926,300
Accumulated Depreciation	(595,800)	(718,200)
Net Book Value	230,500	208,100
Total Assets	$1,465,100	$1,243,278
Bank Notes	$ 286,000	$ —
Accounts Payable	306,000	306,000
Accruals	77,500	77,500
Current Liabilities	$ 669,500	$ 383,500
Mortgage	36,700	36,700
Common Stock	365,000	365,000
Retained Earnings	393,900	458,078
Liabilities + Equity	$1,465,100	$1,243,278

Paley Products, Inc.
Cash Flow Forecast 2002

Sources of Funds

Net Income	$ 64,178
Depreciation	122,400
Decrease in Inventory	237,864
Decrease in Accounts Receivable	65,624
Total Sources of Funds	$490,066

Uses of Funds

Pay Off Bank Debt	$286,000
Capital Expenditures	100,000
Total Uses of Funds	$386,000
Net Increase in Cash	$104,066
Plus Beginning Cash	20,400
Ending Cash Balance	$124,466

Appendix D

Matching Exercise

Exhibit D-1 gives ten sets of ratios and other financial information. The names of ten companies, representing different industries, are given below. Match each set of financial information with the company that produced it.

1. Con Edison: A major power utility based in New York City
2. AIG: A global insurance and related services company
3. Continental Airlines
4. WPP: A global advertising agency
5. Nordstrom: An upscale department store chain, selling mostly clothing
6. Right Associates: A management consulting firm
7. Sara Lee: A food, coffee, and tea company
8. Merck: A pharmaceutical and medical products company
9. A&P: A supermarket chain
10. I.T.T. Educational Services: A nationwide chain of over seventy accredited colleges and technical schools

Exhibit D-1.

Company:	A	B	C	D	E	F	G	H	I	J
Cash and Equivalents	9.0%	3.7%	3.1%	51.1%	30.3%	0.9%	22.0%	11.7%	2.7%	9.2%
Accounts Receivable	11.5%	6.8%	4.2%	8.9%	5.3%	23.1%	—	26.5%	15.7%	28.2%
Inventory	8.0%	23.7%	1.4%	—	3.0%	31.9%	—	—	24.6%	—
Net Fixed Assets	27.2%	54.1%	73.1%	24.4%	51.7%	43.7%	1.0%	4.3%	19.7%	15.3%
Other Assets and Goodwill	44.3%	11.7%	18.2%	15.6%	9.7%	0.4%	77.0%	57.5%	37.3%	47.3%
Total Assets	100.0%	100.0%	100.0%	100.0%	100.0%	100.0%	100.0%	100.0%	100.0%	100.0%
Short-Term Debt	8.0%	4.2%	5.7%	—	3.3%	12.7%	13.8%	1.6%	10.8%	5.0%
Accounts Payable	11.6%	17.5%	4.0%	12.9%	11.0%	11.2%	1.5%	14.4%	16.0%	27.4%
Current Liabilities	24.6%	33.7%	13.5%	51.9%	32.4%	32.8%	15.3%	59.0%	65.2%	35.9%
Long-Term Debt	8.8%	25.9%	20.8%	4.0%	36.7%	11.1%	1.5%	4.1%	18.4%	15.2%
Other Liabilities	29.4%	40.4%	10.1%	—	10.8%	4.9%	70.9%	20.1%	13.5%	2.0%
Stockholders' Equity	37.2%	25.4%	65.6%	44.1%	20.1%	51.2%	12.3%	36.2%	12.6%	46.4%
Total Liabilities + Equity	100.0%	100.0%	100.0%	100.0%	100.0%	100.0%	100.0%	100.0%	100.0%	100.0%

Selected Ratios:

	A	B	C	D	E	F	G	H	I	J
Current Ratio	1.3	1.18	0.82	1.3	0.82	1.71	1.4	—	0.89	1.21
Days' Sales Outstanding	46 days	8.2	31.5	13.5	18.0	44	—	151	36.8	68.0
Inventory Turnover	6.2×	9.2×	7.1×	—	NA	4.2×	—	—	3.4×	—
Debt/Equity	24%	102%	32%	8.0%	182%	0.63	0.89	0.539	2.57	0.327
Return on Equity	44.5%	2.0%	6.8%	40.6%	18.8%	8.65%	15.2%	26.3%	97.1%	15.5%
Return on Assets	16.5%	1.0%	4.5%	17.9%	3.8%	3.07%	1.9%	4.1%	10.5%	7.2%
Revenue/Assets	0.92	3.04	0.48	2.41	1.05	1.67	0.068	0.327	1.58	1.51

Appendix D Answer Key

Here are the companies that match the sets of financial statements. For each company, a few of the ratios and other financial information that should have led you to match the company to the correct set of financial statements are mentioned.

A. Merck

The company has excellent margins and profitability ratios. Days' sales outstanding is high because the company sells to hospitals. It has very little long-term debt and a very comfortable cash level.

B. A & P

Because most of the company's sales are for cash, accounts receivable is very low. Low margins are typical of this industry. The high revenue/assets ratio reflects high inventory turnover, but A&P also owns its own buildings. Food inventory has a very high turnover, but staples do not.

C. Con Edison

As a utility, this company is very fixed-asset-intensive with a reasonably good collection period.

D. I.T.T. Educational Services

This is a very profitable, well-run business. Most funds are collected in advance (tuition), and inventory is nonexistent. The company has low debt and high profitability ratios.

E. Continental Airlines

Airlines are very fixed-asset-intensive. The low level of receivables reflects collections from travel agencies and prepurchase of tickets. Inventory is low because the major part of it is fuel, which is basically purchased when needed. High debt is common among airlines because of the need to finance airplane purchases.

F. Nordstrom

The level of inventory turnover reflects the seasonality of the business. Margins are quite good for a retail operation. Days' sales outstanding reflects self-financing of Nordstrom credit cards.

G. AIG

The company has no inventory or receivables, as premiums are collected in advance. It is very cash-rich (as a result of investments). The high level of nondebt liabilities reflects benefit reserves.

H. WPP Advertising Agency

The company has a very high level of receivables, reflecting the fact that work is billed after it is completed and the difficulty of collecting for an intangible service. High goodwill reflects the acquisition of companies with few tangible assets.

I. Sara Lee

The company has reasonable margins. The high return on equity reflects the high debt/equity ratio and prior years' losses, which reduced equity. The inventory level reflects large raw materials purchases and the fact that much of the finished product is frozen before sale.

J. Right Associates

This company has high receivables because it bills much of its work only after the work is completed. It has no inventory. Other assets are mainly goodwill resulting from acquisitions.

Glossary

10K The annual report that every issuer of public securities, every company whose stock is listed on any stock exchange, and any company with 500 or more shareholders must submit to the Securities and Exchange Commission. The 10K is similar to the annual report that every shareholder receives; it contains a complete set of financial statements and more backup detail, but no photographs or "public relations" type information.

Accelerated Cost Recovery System (ACRS) A depreciation methodology prescribed by the Internal Revenue Service. It has been modified a number of times since it was first introduced; the version currently prescribed is known as the Modified Accelerated Cost Recovery System (MACRS). It shortens the depreciable lives of equipment but provides less than the full straight-line deduction the first year. The depreciable lives prescribed by MACRS are changed frequently as the technological lives of equipment become shorter. The use of MACRS is required by the IRS for tax reporting but is not acceptable under GAAP for financial reporting.

Accounting The reporting of the past in dollars. Accounting records business transactions after they occur. When all of these transactions are recorded, the results are compiled (added up) and summarized in what we know as financial statements.

Accounts Payable   The amount the company owes to its suppliers for products and services that it has already received, but has not yet paid for. Accounts payable is a short-term liability, meaning that it is due in less than one year; it is probably due within 30 to 60 days from the date of the balance sheet.

Accounts Receivable   The amount of money that the company is owed by its customers for products and/or services that it has provided but for which it has not yet been paid. It is a current asset, meaning that it is due in less than one year; it is probably due within 30 to 60 days of the balance sheet date.

Accounts Receivable Financing   A form of borrowing in which the company uses accounts receivable as collateral for loans provided by banks or commercial finance companies.

Accrual Accounting   The accounting methodology used by essentially all public corporations and almost all private companies. With this methodology, revenues are recorded when the money is earned and expenses are recorded when the resource is consumed, without regard to when cash is received or spent. The alternative methodology is doing the accounting on a cash basis. This means that revenue is recorded when the cash is received and expenses are recorded when the bills are actually paid.

Acid Test Ratio (Quick Ratio)   See *Quick Ratio*.

Acquisition   Generally, the purchase of one company by another. The transaction can be for cash, stock, debt, or any combination of these.

Administrative Expenses   What the company spends on its support staff and the infrastructure that that support staff needs in order to contribute to the company's success. Included in the support staff are:

- Accounting
- Legal
- Human resources
- Management information systems

The supporting infrastructure includes such things as:

- The corporate headquarters
- Office supplies
- The computer system

Aging Schedule   A detailed listing of how long the company has been waiting for its customers to pay their bills. This is an analytical tool that helps management to gauge the effectiveness of the company's accounts receivable collection efforts. While days' sales outstanding (DSO) identifies the average age of receivables, it may mask specific problem situations. The aging schedule of a company that sells with 30-day payment requirements might be:

0–30 days	Not yet due
30–45 days	Should be received soon
45–60 days	Indicative of a problem; put on credit watch
60–75 days	Very serious; consider stopping shipments
Above 75 days	Collection in doubt

AICPA   The accountants' professional organization. The initials stand for American Institute of Certified Public Accountants.

Amortization   For investments, the accounting mechanism for apportioning an investment in an intangible asset over the years of its productive (useful) life. Intangibles that are amortized include copyrights, licenses, trademarks, and goodwill. Each year a commensurate share of the whole investment will be included as a noncash expense on the income statement. This concept is very similar to depreciation expense, except that depreciation is for fixed (tangible) assets.

For a loan, an arrangement whereby fixed monthly payments that include principal and interest are calculated. Each payment includes interest for the period and a sufficient amount of principal to retire the loan after the specified number of payments. A loan that is amortized over 20 years will have 240 equal monthly payments.

Angel Financing   A form of venture capital that finances a startup at its earliest stages. The business is probably only an idea at this point. There may be a business plan, but not necessarily. The "angel" is probably a wealthy friend or relative, although it may be a venture capital firm if the idea involves a high-tech concept developed by someone with a track record in the field. The angel provides cash and management expertise in exchange for a portion of the equity.

Asset-Based Lending   Borrowing funds from a bank or other financial institution using the company's assets as collateral for the loan. A home mortgage is a form of asset-based lending that uses real estate as collateral. Working capital loans use accounts receivable and inventory as the collateral asset.

Using assets as collateral is often the only way a smaller business can borrow from a commercial bank. It can also result in lower interest rates and fees because it reduces the lender's risk.

Assets   Those resources owned by the company. These are classified as follows:

Very liquid:
- Cash and cash equivalents
- Short-term marketable securities

Working capital:
- Accounts receivable
- Inventory

Tangible or fixed assets:
- Land
- Buildings
- Machinery and equipment
- Vehicles, furniture, and fixtures

Intangible or financial assets:
- Ownership of other companies
- Other equity or debt investments
- Copyrights
- Patents
- Trademarks
- Goodwill

Audit   A review and critique of the company's accounting system, its control procedures, and the actual accounting process by a disinterested party. The elements reviewed include the recording of events and the preparation of the financial statements. The audit process also involves gaining assurance that the numbers presented in those financial statements are reasonably accurate.

A certified audit is performed by an outside, independent CPA firm that is hired by the stockholders. Such a firm sometimes achieves these objectives by supervising people called "internal auditors." These internal auditors are employees of the company but are supervised by the CPA firm.

Audit Letter (Certification Letter) The letter written by the CPA firm to the stockholders that provides assurance (or creates doubt) that the audit was performed correctly and that there is a reasonable certainty that the financial statements are presented accurately.

The letter appears in the company's annual report and should be read. It alludes to the complexities and uncertainties of the accounting process. It is often the focal point of litigation because of differing views of what it does and does not promise.

Balance Sheet A financial statement prepared by the company at the end of every fiscal period that presents the company's assets, liabilities, and stockholders' equity at a point in time. The balance sheet equation is:

$$\text{Assets} - \text{Liabilities} = \text{Equity}$$

Banker's Acceptance A bank-originated corporate credit instrument that is often used to finance product import activities. It helps the importer to be sure that it will get what it ordered and the seller to be sure that it will be paid when the product is "accepted" by the importer.

Bankruptcy The unhappy experience that results from a company's inability to pay its bills. It can be:

Involuntary, when creditors petition the court to declare the debtor insolvent

Voluntary, when the debtor company files the petition

Under Chapter 7 (of the bankruptcy code), the court appoints a trustee with broad powers to take actions, which usually lead to the liquidation of the firm's assets and cessation of its operations.

Chapter 11 permits the company to continue operating. The company and its creditors will work together to try to salvage the business and their relationships. Payment schedules and settlements are negotiated, and debt is restructured. Creditors will often provide new loans and credit to the company in the hope that it will survive and prosper.

Basis Point A finance and banking term that means 1/100 of one percent. One full percentage point equals 100 basis points. When the Federal Reserve reduces interest rates by $1/2$ percent, it has reduced the rates by 50 basis points.

Bill of Lading The documentation that supports the shipment of products.

Billing Cycle The interval between the times that companies send out invoices. It can be as short as a day or as long as a month. Companies should examine their customers' payment practices and shorten the billing cycle if doing so will accelerate payments. This decision should also reflect the administrative costs of sending out invoices, a cost that frequently may be ignored.

Board of Directors The governing body of a corporation. It is elected by and accountable to the stockholders. It hires the senior executives of the organization (who may also be directors) and holds them accountable for business performance and financial integrity.

Bond A corporate debt security that is sold to the public or by private placement in order to raise funds. The maturity is usually between 5 and 30 years. The coupon rate is the stated rate of interest when the bond is issued. Corporate bonds are usually sold in units of $1,000; a bond that is selling at its face value is said to be selling at par. The price of a bond will often fluctuate in response to market conditions during the years in which the bond is outstanding. However, the corporation is obligated to refund the full par value of the bond at maturity.

Book Value An accounting term that describes the original purchase cost of fixed assets less the accumulated depreciation charged against those assets. In this regard, *book value* and *net book value* are synonymous terms.

The term *book value* is also used to describe the stockholders' equity section of the company's balance sheet. The total amount of equity shown on the balance sheet divided by the number of common shares outstanding is referred to as the *book value per share:*

$$\frac{\text{Stockholders' Equity}}{\text{Common Shares Outstanding}} = \text{Book Value per Share}$$

In stock market analysis, the market price of a share of the common stock is then compared with the book value per share, which is used as a benchmark to establish the "premium" at which the shares are selling.

Breakeven Analysis A financial analysis technique that involves studying the relationships among a product's selling price, variable and fixed costs, and production volume and their cumulative impact on business profitability. The specific formula is:

$$\text{Volume} = \frac{\text{Fixed Cost} + \text{Profit}}{\text{Price per Unit} - \text{Variable Cost per Unit} \atop \text{(Contribution Margin)}}$$

See Chapter 9 for a full discussion of this procedure.

Budget Essentially, a financial process of prioritizing the benefits resulting from business opportunities and the investments required to implement those opportunities. Each year the company undertakes what we shall call the planning process. Management thinks about and plans for the future, and makes strategic, operational, and spending decisions. It basically allocates cash to those departments, projects, markets, and endeavors that it believes will add the most value to the business. When all of these decisions have been made, they are recorded in a document called the budget. Therefore, the budget is essentially a documentation of the planning process. It serves as a record, guide, and standard of performance against which to measure and evaluate future results.

Capital   A generic term that describes the total resources available to the company. It is sometimes used to describe total assets. For example, one might say that a cash-rich company is "well capitalized." This means that the company has adequate resources to finance its future. A company that is undercapitalized is one that does not have adequate resources.

Capital Assets   Usually synonymous with fixed or tangible assets. This includes:

> Land
> Buildings
> Machinery and equipment
> Furniture and fixtures
> Vehicles

Capital Budget   The portion of the budget process in which management focuses specifically on the company's fixed asset needs.

Capital Expenditure   The expenditure or disbursement of funds for the purpose of purchasing fixed assets.

Capital Gain   The delightful experience that results from selling an asset held for more than one year at a profit. Revisions in tax laws keep the exact definition of short- and long-term capital gains changing, but the concept does not change.

Capital Lease   A long-term contract in which the lessee or user of a fixed asset essentially assumes ownership, along with possession. The issues considered in deciding whether a lease is in fact a capital lease are:

- The life of the asset compared to the life of the lease
- Transfer of title
- Existence of an option to purchase the asset at a bargain price
- The total amount of lease payments compared with the market value of the asset

If the structure and terms of the lease meet certain criteria, the lessee or user may have to include the asset on the company's balance sheet even though the company does not technically "own" it.

Capital Stock   Common stock of the company.

Capital Structure   The proportions in which the company's assets are financed by lenders (debt) and by stockholders (equity). It addresses, conceptually, whether the company has too much risk (debt) and the degree to which the owners have invested (common stock) and reinvested (retained earnings) in the business.

Capitalization   Defined as long-term debt plus stockholders' equity.

Cash Flow   The overall amount of cash generated by the company that is available to the company to manage the business. It is sometimes also expressed as:

$$\begin{aligned} &\text{Net Income} \\ +\ &\text{Depreciation} \\ =\ &\text{Cash Flow} \end{aligned}$$

Cash Flows, Statement of   A required financial statement in every annual report and 10K. It provides a summary of all cash flows generated and used, categorized as:

- Operating activities
- Investing activities
- Financing activities

Cash Management   A company's operation of the payment and collections functions. This can include short-term investing. The goal is to accelerate the receipt of cash, wisely disburse funds to the company's advantage, and achieve interest income while minimizing administrative expenses.

Certificate of Deposit (CD)   An investment security issued by a commercial or other bank. The denominations of these securities can be as little as $1,000 or as large as millions of dollars. Companies often buy these securities as investments because they provide quite good interest income and are relatively safe. Their maturity can be as short as one month or as long as many years.

Certified Public Accountant (CPA) A person who is well trained in GAAP and related accounting matters and has passed state CPA exams. CPAs are licensed to provide audit, tax, and other accounting advisory services to companies as an independent, disinterested party.

Chief Financial Officer (CFO) The top financial executive in the company. The CFO is responsible for all treasury, controllership, and regulatory compliance functions. As the chief financial analyst for the company, this person can be a valued business adviser to the entire management team.

COGS See *Cost of Goods Sold.*

Collateral Assets pledged as security for a loan. If payments are not made, the creditor can take possession of the assets and sell them to satisfy the debt. A house is collateral on a home mortgage. If there is specific collateral on a loan, the bank or other creditor is described as a *secured lender.*

Collection The process of ensuring that customers who owe the company funds for products and services that the company provided pay in a timely manner. The process also includes processing payments received and depositing the funds in a bank rapidly.

Commercial Loan Funds borrowed from a commercial bank. Commercial loans are usually short-term, covering seasonal needs, large orders, and other temporary cash requirements.

Commercial Paper Promissory notes issued by very large, high-quality corporations. Commercial banks often purchase these investment-grade securities from their client companies in lieu of making a commercial loan. Large industrial corporations sometimes purchase these securities, as do investment companies and mutual funds. Their maturity is always short-term. Because the buyer has a high-quality negotiable instrument, the interest rate is often below the prime rate.

Common Stock Shares of ownership in a corporation. Owners of the shares usually have the right to vote for members of the board of directors and on other issues, although some companies' stock does not have a one-share, one-vote relationship. The dollar amount of common stock shown on the balance sheet is the historical amount that the owners paid when they purchased the stock from the company.

Compensating Balance A minimum balance that bank loan clients must maintain in their checking accounts at all times. Because not all of the amount borrowed is available to the borrowing company, the existence of a compensating balance results in an interest rate that is considerably higher than the stated loan rate.

Completed Contract Method An accounting procedure used for long-term, multiperiod contracts in which the profit achieved is not recognized until the work is completed. The completed contract method is usually used in the construction industry and by defense contractors.

Consideration Something of value that is provided by a party to a contract. Consideration is an essential part of every contract; each party must provide something of value (consideration) for the contract to be valid. A very common form of consideration is cash.

Consignment Sale A method of selling products in which the vendor (the consignor) places its products on the premises of a customer entity (the consignee). Although the consignee possesses the product and must assure its safety, it remains the property of the consignor. When the product is sold to a third party, it becomes the property of that purchaser and is subject to whatever credit terms were agreed upon. This method is most common in a retail environment, especially when the product's marketability is unproven.

Contribution Margin The price of the product less the variable cost to produce it. This term is sometimes used interchangeably with the terms *gross margin* and *gross profit*. It may be expressed on a per-unit basis or be given for the entire product line in dollar or percentage terms.

Convertible Securities Bonds or preferred shares issued by a company that can be exchanged for common shares under certain terms and conditions.

Correspondent Bank A bank that serves as a depository or provides check clearing or other services for smaller commercial banks.

Cost Accounting The accounting practice of measuring the cost incurred to produce a unit of product by cost element—direct labor, direct materials, and supporting overhead.

Cost Allocation   An accounting methodology in which a portion of manufacturing overhead is charged to each unit of product that passes through the facility. The mathematical apportionment may be based on:

- Units of production
- Labor hours
- Pounds of material inputs
- Machine hours

Cost allocation is required by GAAP accounting and is built into the standard cost system. It is also called absorption accounting. The portion of the overhead charged to each unit is often called the *burden.*

Cost of Goods Sold (COGS)   The cost of producing the products that are delivered to customers to create revenue. In a manufacturing company, COGS would include:

- Direct labor: The amounts paid to the people who actually create and assemble the product
- Materials: The cost of all the inventory that goes into the product
- Manufacturing overhead: Some portion of the spending that supports the assembly process

Credit Department   The department that qualifies and monitors the creditworthiness of customers, sends out invoices, and does the accounting for customer collections. It is usually part of the controller's office.

Current Assets   The assets on the balance sheet that are expected to become cash within one year from the date of that balance sheet. These assets include:

- Cash
- Marketable securities
- Accounts receivable

- Inventory
- Prepaid expenses

Current Liabilities   The liabilities of the company that are due within one year from the date of the balance sheet. They include:

- Accounts payable
- Bank debt
- Current portion of long-term debt

Current Portion of Long-Term Debt   Liabilities that had a maturity of more than one year when the funds were originally borrowed, but that now, because of the passage of time, are due in less than one year. It is similar to the principal portion of the next twelve monthly payments on your home mortgage.

Current Ratio   A measure of corporate liquidity. It is calculated as:

$$\frac{\text{Current Assets}}{\text{Current Liabilities}} = \text{Current Ratio}$$

Current Yield   The rate of interest earned on the purchase price of a bond, whether or not the bond is purchased at face value. The formula is:

$$\frac{\text{Annual Interest Income}}{\text{Purchase Price of the Bond}} = \text{Current Yield}$$

Days' Sales Outstanding   A measure of how much time, on average, is being required for the company to receive the cash it has earned from its customers. The time begins when the invoice is sent and ends when the check is received.

$$\frac{\text{Annual Revenue}}{365} = \text{Average Revenue per Day}$$

$$\frac{\text{Accounts Receivable}}{\text{Average Revenue per Day}} = \text{Days' Sales Outstanding}$$

Debenture   A type of corporate bond secured only by the full
faith and credit of the debtor company, not by specific collateral. In a bankruptcy, holders of these bonds would be
general creditors.

Debt Amortization   See *Amortization.*

Debt/Equity Ratio

$$\frac{\text{Long-Term Debt}}{\text{Stockholders' Equity}} = \text{Debt/Equity Ratio}$$

This is a measure of risk for both the company and its current and future creditors.

Debtor   A person or company that owes money to another.

Deferred Charges   An asset account, sometimes part of "other
assets." This is an accumulation account into which payments for future benefits are placed. These cash outlays will
be converted into expenses gradually as the operations
begin. Examples are start-up costs of a new business and up-
front fees associated with stock and bond offerings.

Deferred Revenue   A short- or long-term (or both) liability on
a company's balance sheet. It results from the company's
receiving payments in advance for services or products that
have not yet been provided. The company now "owes" that
amount of services or products to its customer. This "debt"
will be satisfied when those services or products are provided. For example, a magazine subscription results in deferred revenue for the publisher because the payment is
received in advance; it will be converted into actual revenue
as issues of the magazine are delivered.

Deferred Taxes   Tax liabilities of the company. Most companies
pay less in taxes in any one year than the corporate income
tax rate because of differences between the accounting
methodology used in the published financial statements and
that used in filings with the IRS. The difference between the
two amounts, deferred income taxes, appears as a current
liability and/or a long-term debt on the company's balance
sheet. An increase in this liability is evidence that the company actually paid less in taxes than is indicated in the income statement. Notice that on the income statement, the

caption reads "Provision for income taxes" and represents 34 percent of the pretax amount. Most companies' actual tax rate is in the 20 to 25 percent range.

Demand Deposit Funds on deposit in a bank that the owner of the funds can withdraw without notice. The owner of the funds may access these funds easily, usually by writing a check. A checking account in a commercial bank is a common example of a demand deposit.

Demand Loan A bank loan that has no fixed maturity. The loan must be repaid "on demand," meaning that the lender can "demand" the funds from the borrower without notice or reason.

Depreciation A noncash expense that results from the apportionment of a capital expenditure over the useful life of the asset. It is the prime example of the concept that an expense and an expenditure are not the same.

Direct Costs Those costs of producing a product or service that are absolutely essential if the product is to be made or the service to be provided. In creating a product, the labor that makes the product and the material that becomes the product are true direct costs. Some supporting costs in the factory are also classified as direct in a company's standard cost system.

Dividend A payment to holders of preferred and common shares. Dividends are usually a distribution of net income.

Dividend Payout Ratio The portion of net income that is paid to shareholders as a dividend.

$$\frac{\text{Dividend Payment}}{\text{Net Income}} = \text{Payout Ratio}$$

Due Diligence Conceptually, ensuring that the information that was presented is true. Before making a loan, a bank does "due diligence" to make certain that the collateral (receivables, inventory, or real estate) is actually worth the stated value. In the acquisition of another company, the buyer does due diligence to make certain that the seller's representations are accurate and that the buyer's company is getting what it paid for. This is very similar to a home inspection before the closing.

Earnings per Share (EPS)   The portion of the company's net income that is attributable to each share of outstanding common stock. It is calculated as follows:

$$\frac{\text{Net Income} - \text{Preferred Dividends}}{\text{Common Shares Outstanding}} = \text{Earnings per Share}$$

Earnings per Share (EPS) Fully Diluted   A calculation of earnings per share that includes the following in the number of common shares outstanding:

> Earned or vested stock options that have not yet been exercised
> Shares that would result from conversion of any convertible securities

Primary earnings per share is the EPS calculated without including the effects of potential dilution.

EBIT   Earnings before interest and taxes.

EBITDA   Earnings before interest, taxes, and depreciation and amortization. This is the equivalent of operating income on a cash basis.

Economic Order Quantity (EOQ)   The amount of product that the company should buy each time it makes a purchase. Buying in massive quantities will probably reduce purchase cost per unit but will increase inventory, inventory risk, warehouse expense, and financial carrying costs. Buying only the minimum amount needed will reduce those inventory-related costs and the related risk. It will, however, result in increased purchase cost per unit and make the company more vulnerable to stock-outs. EOQ techniques assist management in balancing these issues to identify the most efficient amount to purchase at one time and how frequently to make these purchases.

The way this quantity is calculated is changing because of the technological connection between customer and supplier. But the concept still has validity.

Electronic Data Interchange (EDI) A computerized connection between customer and supplier that permits more economic control of inventory and more efficient supply chain management.

Electronic Payments Transfers of cash between banks that are accomplished without the actual writing of checks. Float is essentially eliminated because checks need not clear. Direct deposit of your payroll check is an excellent example of this.

Escrow Money or other property held by a disinterested party, known as an escrow agent, until the conditions of a contract are fulfilled. The closing on a house is an escrow process, especially when funds are held for a while after the meeting because one of the parties has not satisfied all of the conditions.

Factoring Selling accounts receivable to a third party, usually a bank factoring department or a finance company. The credit risk can be sold with the paper (factoring without recourse) or be kept by the company until the funds are collected (factoring with recourse). This is a very expensive form of financing. It is often used by clothing manufacturers and distributors.

FASB Financial Accounting Standards Board. A professional accounting organization that researches accounting and reporting issues and recommends revisions to accounting and reporting rules. The products of the FASB's efforts are called *FASB Bulletins.*

Federal Funds Rate Interest rate charged by banks when they lend to each other.

Federal Reserve System An independent agency of the executive branch of the U.S. government that is responsible, among other things, for regulating many activities of commercial banks. Through its monitoring of the money supply, it has vast influence on interest rates and on overall economic and business activity. The Federal Reserve System has a board of governors in Washington, D.C., and thirteen regional banks that focus on issues relating to the economies of their respective regions.

Finance Charge Interest payments on borrowed funds and the related fees for arranging the loans.

Finance Company   A private, for-profit organization that lends money to companies. It may originate those loans on behalf of banks or actually make the loans itself. These loans can then be sold to banks or other finance companies. Finance companies often function as factors.

Fiscal Year   An accounting year. It may or may not coincide with the calendar year.

Fixed Assets   Assets owned by the company and used in the operation of its business that are expected to last more than one year; also called tangible assets. They include:

- Land and buildings
- Machinery and equipment
- Furniture and fixtures
- Vehicles

All of these assets except land are subject to depreciation.

Fixed Costs   Costs that a company incurs that are not directly sensitive to volume changes.

Float   Funds in transit between banks. From the time a check is written and sent until the receiver deposits the check and the check clears, neither the sender nor the receiver has the use of the money. The depository bank has free use of the money until the check clears. No corporation can write a check on funds that have not yet cleared.

Footnotes   That section of the annual report (or any financial statement package) that provides greater detail than the financial statements themselves. The notes describe various accounting procedures and policies, and provide considerable critical backup information necessary for understanding the financial statements.

Foreign Currency Translation   Gains and losses that the company experiences on investments and debts that are denominated in foreign currency as a result of changes in the value of that foreign currency relative to the dollar.

Freight on Board (FOB)   The concept that determines exactly when title to goods that have been shipped transfers to the recipient. FOB Origin means that the receiver owns and is responsible for the product from the time it leaves the seller's premises. FOB Destination means that the shipper remains responsible until the product reaches the customer.

General and Administrative Expense   All the staff expenses and other supporting expenses necessary to operate the business. Among the many expenses included might be:

- Building rent
- Staff salaries
- Costs of operating the accounting and legal departments

General Ledger   The summary set of accounting books that contains consolidated information on each account. The general ledger serves as the basis for the preparation of financial statements.

Generally Accepted Accounting Principles (GAAP)   The general principles and rules that govern the efforts of the accounting profession. Their focus is on the way in which accounting information is prepared and reported.

Goodwill   The amount of money that the company paid to acquire other companies in excess of the value of the tangible assets acquired as part of the transaction. This accounting definition of goodwill is not at all related to the more common use of the term to describe the market value of the company's reputation. Goodwill appears as a long-term asset on the company's balance sheet.

Gross Margin

> Revenue
> − Cost of Goods Sold
> = Gross Margin

Gross margin is sometimes called, but is not necessarily always the same as, gross profit.

Hurdle Rate   The minimum ROI that companies require before they will approve a capital expenditure proposal.

Income Statement   A report of revenues, expenses, and profit that describes a company's performance during a fiscal period.

Indirect Costs   Costs that are not attributable to a single area but support the entirety of the business.

Industrial Revenue Bond   A long-term bond issued by a municipal government on the behalf of a company. The proceeds are loaned to the company for the purpose of facilities expansion and, more importantly (from the government's point of view), job creation. The government agency usually sells the bond to a bank. The use of these bonds provides tax advantages for the investor, interest rate benefits for the company, and job creation opportunities for the municipality.

Initial Public Offering (IPO)   The first offering of a company's common stock to the public. It requires registration with the Securities and Exchange Commission and is usually underwritten by investment bankers.

Insolvency   A serious financial condition resulting from a company's inability to pay its bills. It often results in bankruptcy.

Installment Credit   Loans that are repaid through fixed periodic payments of principal and interest.

Institute of Management Accountants   A professional and educational association whose membership includes accountants and financial analysts.

Intangible Assets   Assets that cannot be seen or touched but may have considerable value. Evidence of these assets may literally be only a piece of paper. Examples are investments in other companies, licenses, copyrights, and trademarks.

Interest   The fee paid to a lender for funds borrowed.

Internal Rate of Return   The actual return on investment (ROI) based upon the discounted cash flow method of investment analysis. Using time value of money concepts, it is calculated by equalizing the present value of the cash inflows (PVCI) and the present value of the cash outflows (PVCO). The formula, which appears in all computer software that calculates ROI, is:

$$PVCO = PVCI \times F\ (\%, yrs)$$

where F is the present value factor corresponding to the ROI percentage (%) and the number of years in the project forecast (yrs).

Internal Revenue Service (IRS) The part of the Treasury Department of the U.S. government that is responsible for the administration and collection of taxes and the enforcement of the tax laws as prescribed by Congress.

Inventory The financial investment that the company has made in the manufacture or production (or, in the case of a retail store, the purchase) of products that will be sold to customers. There are two primary methods of accounting for Inventory:

LIFO, or last-in, first-out
FIFO, or first-in, first-out

Invoice A notification to a customer that the customer owes the company money for products and services provided. It may contain some details of the sale and certainly should communicate a due date.

Lease A contract to obtain the use of an asset over an extended period of time. This often results in the lessee (user) owning the asset after the lease ends.

Lender A provider of loans.

Lessee The party that leases an asset from the owner, who is the lessor.

Letter of Credit A bank document issued on behalf of the buyer of a product that guarantees that the seller will be paid upon delivery of the product. This eliminates the seller's credit risk. Letters of credit are often used in international transactions. They are a form of banker's acceptance.

Letter of Intent A document, bordering on a contractual promise, that specifies certain actions that will be taken by the writer if certain conditions are met. Banks write letters of intent before they make loans, and buyers of businesses may write such a letter before entering the due diligence process.

Leverage (Financial) The use of borrowed funds to expand the business and increase its profitability.

Leveraged Buyout The use of the assets being purchased as collateral for the loan that will finance that purchase. The term is usually applied to the purchase of a company; however, conceptually, the purchase of a house is also a leveraged buyout, as the collateral for the loan is the house being purchased. The collateral must be of high quality, and the borrower's ability to repay the loan needs to be demonstrated.

Lien   An attachment of an asset, often used as collateral for a loan. The lien can be involuntary, resulting from a borrower's inability to pay bills.

Line of Credit   Arranging for a loan in advance of the time the funds are required. This ensures that they will be available if and when they are needed. It saves interest expense because the funds are not actually borrowed until they are required.

The existence of a line of credit demonstrates the company's borrowing power and financial strength. Information about the company's lines of credit is often found in the footnotes of a public company's annual report.

Liquidity   The ability of the company to pay its bills on a regular basis and maintain the working capital levels necessary to support the business.

Lockbox   A payment mechanism. Customers send their payments to a post office box located near the company's bank. The bank collects the payments from the box and deposits them in the company's checking account. The company is then immediately notified of the deposit by the bank. This accelerates the clearing process, reduces float, and increases the company's interest income.

London Interbank Offered Rate (LIBOR)   A benchmark interest rate that is used in many contracts and variable-rate loans. It is the interest rate that European banks charge each other for interbank loans. It is very similar to the American federal funds rate.

Long-Term Debt   Borrowed funds that are not due until more than one year from the date of the balance sheet.

Lower of Cost or Market   An accounting principle that governs the reporting of assets on the company's balance sheet. Assets are presented at their historical cost or their current market value, whichever is lower. GAAP rules do not permit reflection of improved market value of assets on certified financial statements.

Management Discussion and Analysis   A critical, required section of a company's annual report to shareholders. It is a letter from management, usually the CEO, that identifies, describes, and comments on all of the critical events of the past year that had a material effect on the past performance or anticipated future performance of the company.

Maturity Date   The date on which loans are required to be repaid.

Mezzanine Financing   Financing that companies use on an interim basis pending a stock issue or refinancing. Since it is often subordinated to other debt, it will usually have a higher interest rate.

Milestone Accounting   A method of recognizing revenue and billing the customer during a multiperiod contract. When the product is delivered, its value, and therefore the amount of the invoice, is readily determinable. In a long-term contract such as a construction contract, however, identifying when money is earned is not as clear. In milestone accounting, the company and the customer establish a predetermined series of events, the achievement of which permits the company to bill. These milestones might occur monthly or be based upon some other measure of completion.

Minority Shareholders   Shareholders who own too few shares to have any control over or influence on the activities of management or the future of the company.

Mortgage Bonds   Long-term debt of the company that is secured by specific assets, usually real estate.

Net Book Value   See *Book Value.*

Net Income   Bottom-line profit, recorded after all costs, expenses, and taxes have been subtracted from revenue.

Net Present Value   The present value of the cash inflows from an investment minus the present value of the cash outflows; a discounted cash flow measure for evaluating an investment. A positive net present value indicates that the investment opportunity being measured is more profitable than the company's minimum ROI requirement.

Note, Promissory   A written agreement to repay a debt plus interest at a certain date or on demand.

Operating Income   A company's profit before one-time events,

other income and expenses, and corporate taxes. It is usually
defined as:

> Revenue
> − Cost of Goods Sold
> = Gross Profit
> − Selling, General, and Administrative Expenses
> − Depreciation and Amortization
> = Operating Income

Operating Lease   A contract giving the lessee the use of a fixed
asset for a relatively short period of time. The lessee or user
assumes little or no responsibility for the asset and has no
intention of buying it. Renting a car at the airport for two
days is an operating lease.

Operating Margin   A company's operating income as a percentage of revenue:

$$\frac{\text{Operating Income}}{\text{Revenue}} = \text{Operating Margin \%}$$

This is a measure of a company's operating performance. It
is widely used and is an excellent measure of profit center
performance.

Outsourcing   Hiring outside people or another company to accomplish work or produce product. Buying components
from a supplier for in-house assembly is "outsourcing" the
production of those components. Hiring a law firm, an insurance consultant, or computer software developers for
specific projects are all forms of outsourcing. The company
usually gets better expertise than what it can afford internally and does not end up with unneeded employees after
the project is completed.

Overdraft Account   An account at a commercial bank that gives
the company the privilege of writing checks for more than
its balance. It is essentially a line of credit attached to the
account that gives the company some cash flexibility and
ensures that its checks will not bounce.

Overhead   Costs of doing business that are not directly related to the actual manufacturing process. This includes all costs for the corporate staff. Conceptually, there is considerable overlap between overhead and general and administrative expenses.

Paid-In Capital   The total amount that the shareholders have invested in the company in either common or preferred stock in excess of the par value of the shares. Many companies' stock does not have a par value. Therefore, these companies do not have any paid-in capital. The par value of common or preferred stock has no operational or stock market significance, with the exception that it might become important if the company should become bankrupt.

Par Value   A nominal or face value given to a bond or share of stock. Par for a bond is usually $1,000. Par value for a common share is a purely arbitrary amount. It has no relation to what the price was when the shares were originally sold or to their current market value.

Performance Bond   A form of insurance purchased by the party to a contract who is undertaking to do some work; it provides a guarantee to the other party that the work will be done. It offers financial assurance and protection if terms of the contract are not fulfilled.

Preferred Dividend   Distribution of a portion of net income to the holders of preferred shares. Like all dividends, these dividends are not tax-deductible for the company.

Preferred Stock   A hybrid class of stockholders' equity. Owners of these shares receive a dividend that, unless the company is in financial distress, is essentially fixed. They do not normally have the right to vote (for the board of directors), but they have priority in receiving dividends in that their dividends must be paid before anything can be paid to the holders of common shares.

Prepaid Expenses   Expenses that are paid before the time period that will benefit. For example, insurance premiums might be paid in advance at six-month intervals. The payment is a current asset on the balance sheet. The amount paid is then amortized, with one-sixth of the amount being charged to each of the monthly periods as an expense.

Price/Earnings Ratio   The relationship between the price of a company's stock and the company's earnings per share:

$$\frac{\text{Common Stock Price}}{\text{Earnings per Share}} = \text{Price/Earnings Ratio}$$

To the extent that the stock market is a rational business, the price/earnings ratio reflects the market's perception of the company's future prospects for earnings growth. The higher the ratio, the more positive is the market's outlook for the stock.

Prime Rate   The interest rate that commercial banks charge on loans to their largest, most creditworthy customers.

Principal   The face amount of any debt, without inclusion of future interest payments.

Pro Forma Statement   A financial statement that incorporates information other than actual accounting information. A budget is a pro forma statement, as is a forecast.

Profit Center   An independent organization within a company that has a readily identifiable market and core competencies. Its performance is usually measured by its revenues, expenses, and profitability. The profit center is often responsible for the assets that are available for its use.

Property, Plant, and Equipment   A term that is usually synonymous with fixed assets. It is sometimes used to refer to the gross book value, and at other times to the net book value.

Quick Assets   Cash and near-cash assets, including short-term marketable securities and accounts receivable.

Quick Ratio   A ratio that assists management in assessing the company's liquidity position. The formula is:

$$\frac{\text{Cash} + \text{Marketable Securities} + \text{Accounts Receivable}}{\text{Accounts Payable} + \text{Bank Debt}}$$

$$= \text{Acid Test/Quick Ratio}$$

This ratio basically compares near-cash assets with current liabilities (those that are due within the next year). The ratio differs from the current ratio in that inventory is excluded. Finished goods inventory still has to be sold and delivered.

Raw materials and work in process inventory require additional effort and expenditure just to be completed. So in terms of their ability to be turned into cash, there is a wide gap between accounts receivable and inventory.

Because service businesses have little or no inventory, their quick and current ratios will be the same.

Ratio A mathematical comparison of two or more numbers. It assists management in evaluating some area of company performance. A ratio can be fully financial, such as return on equity (ROE), or statistical, such as capacity utilization or order backlog.

Reserves Allowances for future negative events. Accounting requires recognition of bad news as soon as the possibility arises, but permits recognition of good news only after it actually occurs.

One example of a reserve is the allowance for bad debts. A company knows that its accounts receivable are sometimes not 100 percent collectible. It statistically determines that, over time, 1 percent of its funds have not been fully collected. Therefore, the company creates a reserve in the amount of 1 percent of accounts receivable, the allowance for bad debts, which is subtracted from accounts receivable on the balance sheet. Another type of reserve would be set up by a retail store that has Christmas products left over in January. Knowing that the product will have to be sold at below normal prices, it will create a reserve for the estimated losses that it will experience on this sale.

Retained Earnings The cumulative amount of the company's net income that the owners have reinvested in the business during its entire corporate history. It is part of stockholders' equity on the balance sheet. Corporate net income can either be retained or be paid out as dividends to holders of preferred and common shares. The cumulative total of the amounts not paid out as dividends is the Retained Earnings account on the balance sheet.

Return on Equity A ratio that measures the overall performance of the company. It reflects profitability, efficiency, and the effective use of debt. The ratio is traditionally:

$$\frac{\text{Net Income}}{\text{Stockholders' Equity}} = \text{Return on Equity (ROE)}$$

Rollover   A delay in making principal payments on a loan. It could be a positive action to extend the duration of existing loans for a longer period, or it could take place because the debtor does not have the cash to make the payments. The bank will dictate the terms of the rollover if it is necessitated by debtor weakness. Alternatively, a strong company may make a rollover a condition of a future client relationship with the bank. The connotation of the term *rescheduling* is almost always debtor weakness.

Sales   A very vague, often misinterpreted term. *Revenue* is a precise concept; it is the amount recorded on the income statement when the company earns money by providing products and services to the customer. Sales sometimes means revenue. It can also mean customer orders, which are not yet revenue. If the production operation is busy, some might say that "sales are going well." "Business is excellent" might mean that there are many customer inquiries. This is not sales (orders), deliveries (revenue), or cash (collections).

Secured Loan   Borrowing funds using specific assets as collateral for the loan. A mortgage is a secured loan because real estate is pledged as collateral. Accounts receivable financing is another form of secured loan. In a bankruptcy, a secured lender has first priority on the pledged asset to satisfy the debt before the remainder of the proceeds become available to the general (unsecured) creditors.

Securities and Exchange Commission (SEC)   A U.S. government agency with oversight responsibility for the securities industry. Among its many responsibilities, it specifies the substance of a public company's annual report and 10K, oversees the fairness of stock trading, and monitors insiders' buying and selling of their company's shares.

Standard Cost System   An accounting mechanism that provides information necessary to determine how much it costs the company to produce its products. It requires definite assumptions concerning volumes, efficiency, and product mix. In a manufacturing environment, it is the basis for the accounting system.

Stock Option A contract that gives the owner the right to purchase a predetermined number of shares of a company's stock at a specified price. It is a very common form of executive compensation at public companies. Earned options are part of the dilution effect in the company's earnings per share calculation.

Subordinated Debenture A corporate bond on which, should the company issuing it have financial difficulties become bankrupt, the payment of interest and repayment of principal will have a lower priority than the payment of interest and repayment of principal on senior debentures.

Supply Chain Management The strategies associated with sourcing and receiving purchased products and the related management of raw material and components inventory. Technological advances have drastically improved information and communication, leading to lower inventories and improved efficiency at all phases of the process.

Term Loan A long-term debt; traditionally, one that has a maturity of one to five years.

Three Cs of Credit: Capacity, Collateral, Character The traditional criteria that bankers use when evaluating a loan application.

Treasury Management The entire range of responsibilities for cash within a company. Among the treasurer's many responsibilities are cash collections, the mobilization of the funds into usable form, investment of funds, and also future planning.

Treasury Stock Company stock that was issued to the public and subsequently repurchased by the company on the open market. In the equity section of the balance sheet, the stock appears as negative shares outstanding at the cost of the repurchase rather than the current market value. Once treasury stock has been purchased, it can be retired to improve earnings per share or held for resale later.

Variable Costs Costs that a company incurs that will be significantly affected by changes in production volume. For example, the number of workers necessary to produce the product will certainly be affected by how much product needs to be produced. The amount of material, components, and parts needed will fluctuate with volume on a direct cause-and-effect basis. Therefore, these are variable costs.

Venture Capital A form of financing used in the early stages of a company's life. At best, the company being financed probably has little or no track record and products that are not yet market-proven. Or the company may be at a still earlier stage; it may have developed a business plan and product prototype, or it may be only an idea. This is a highly speculative and risky form of investing.

Warrant A security giving the holder the right to buy stock in the company. Stock options are given to employees, whereas warrants are often given to lenders or investors as an inducement to do a transaction. Options are nontransferable, whereas warrants may have an independent value and may also be marketable securities.

Working Capital A term usually used to refer to cash and other current assets such as marketable securities, accounts receivable, and inventory. Sometimes working capital is defined as being synonymous with current assets. Other times, it is defined as:

$$\text{Current Assets} - \text{Current Liabilities} = \text{Working Capital}$$

The term is sometimes used as a generalized reference to a company's overall liquidity condition. For example, someone might say, "The company has adequate working capital," meaning that it has adequate cash-related assets to run the business.

Zero-Based Budgeting A budgeting philosophy and technique that requires a company to regularly rethink and reevaluate all aspects of how it conducts its business. It was first promulgated in a *Harvard Business Review* article and was made famous by then Governor Jimmy Carter of Georgia.

Technology has made it possible to include this concept in our regular annual budget process. Having become comfortable with change, companies do rethink their ways of doing business. They outsource less important, resource-consuming activities and focus on their core competencies. This was the basis of zero-based budgeting: It deemphasized last year's spending in developing the current year's budget requirements.

Zero-Coupon Bond   A corporate bond that pays no annual cash interest but is sold at a discount from face value such that, if the bond is held to maturity, it will yield the indicated, competitively priced, interest rate. During its life, the price of this bond will fluctuate in accordance with market conditions. As it gets closer to maturity, the bond price will gravitate toward its face amount. A U.S. savings bond is a form of zero-coupon bond.

Index